The Presence of the Past

University of Florida Monographs
Social Sciences No. 57

The Presence of the Past

John Dewey and Alfred Schutz
on the
Genesis and Organization of Experience

Rodman B. Webb

A University of Florida Book

The University Presses of Florida
Gainesville

Library of Congress Cataloging in Publication Data

Webb, Rodman B. 1941–
   The presence of the past.

   (University of Florida monographs: Social sciences;
no. 57)
   "A University of Florida book."
   Bibliography: p.
   1. Dewey, John, 1859–1952. 2. Schutz, Alfred, 1899–
1959. 3. Experience. 4. Relevance (Philosophy)
I. Title. II. Series: Florida. University, Gainesville. University of Florida monographs: Social sciences; no. 57.
B945.D44W39   128   76-25461
ISBN 0–8130–0560–4

Second printing, 1978

TYPOGRAPHY BY MODERN TYPOGRAPHERS, INCORPORATED
CLEARWATER, FLORIDA

PRINTED BY STORTER PRINTING COMPANY, INCORPORATED
GAINESVILLE, FLORIDA

Preface

SOME social scientists have lost their way, because they blindly follow paths cut by colleagues in the physical sciences. Others have gone astray because they abandoned science altogether. As a result, social science—perhaps in an effort to find itself—has lost sight of man, the subject of its study. Only through a metatheoretical examination of human experience will social science regain its bearings. John Dewey and Alfred Schutz can give clearer direction to such an examination. This study attempts to organize and underline some of what they have to offer. Neither Dewey nor Schutz finds answers to all the problems that are shrouded in the mystery of human experience; however, they clarify many of them. "Of my results I am not so sure," said Schutz. "Others may do better; but of one thing I am deeply convinced. *Here* are the problems of the social sciences."

This study began in courses taught by Peter Berger at Rutgers University. It developed into a dissertation under the direction of James E. Wheeler. After further work, it took its present form. More people than I can acknowledge and thank properly have helped along the way. I am indebted particularly to the thoughtful criticism of my father, Jean Francis Webb, who said of this work, "What it lacks in plot it more than makes up for in humor." I am also grateful to Mrs. Alfred Schutz for her invaluable cooperation. Special thanks go to Michele Lepore and James Giarelli, who doggedly tracked down footnotes and gave other editorial assistance. It is impossible to thank adequately my wife, Elise: what she has taught me of human experience is a special contribution.

Contents

1. The Retreat from Experience

Experience is never a static affair, despite substantial philosophical and scientific efforts to treat it as such. The facts of human experience resist rigid models of man that deny consciousness or render it simply a repetitive instrument. Change is integral to human action; all models of man must ultimately come to terms with that. Human events are inherently precarious, and this fact remains whether or not we choose to recognize it. Man must base his actions on imperfect anticipations, judgments, and beliefs which, John Dewey tells us, "can never attain more than a precarious probability." For this reason, "the distinctive characteristic of practical activity, one which is so inherent that it cannot be eliminated, is the uncertainty which attends it."[1]*

The history of philosophy could be approached through studying man's effort to escape the nagging discomfort of doubt. Dewey's *Quest for Certainty* shows clearly how philosophies have developed elaborate systems of thought and theoretical legerdemain to disprove the humbling fact that man will never know all there is to know, and that tomorrow's discoveries may well render today's certainties trivial, or worse, absurd. Much of philosophy has worked to discover fixed truths, immutable first principles which would guarantee lasting order to a troubled world. In this effort, philosophy was doomed to failure from the start.

Dewey retraced philosophy to its beginning in the primitive world. There, he contended, "the precarious crises of birth, puberty, illness, death, war, famine, plague, the uncertainties of the hunt, the vicissitudes of climate and the great seasonal changes, kept imagination occupied with the uncertain."[2] Religion was born in this context.

---

* Notes begin on p. 111. In order to provide readily available sources, citations whenever possible are to current collections of articles and essays or to low-cost paperback editions.

Dewey believed that early religion offered man an immediate, two-story vision of the world. One level belonged to man, uncertainty, and worldly objects; the other to perfection, essences, and certitude. The world of perfection began to be seen as a different order from that of everyday life, known only through rituals, magic, and through priests endowed with other-worldly powers. The mechanics of daily living were untrustworthy, mercurial, illusory, and thus hardly worth knowing at all.

Although anthropological data would place this division later in the development of religion,[3] Dewey has clearly read its significance. Western philosophy, he said, inherited from religion "the idea of a higher realm of fixed reality . . . and of an inferior world of changing things with which experience and practical matters are concerned." While philosophy substituted the rational for magic and ritual, it directed attention not to the activities of man but to the search for immutable and antecedent truth. Dewey explained that this merely "translated into a rational form the doctrine of escape from the vicissitudes of existence by means . . . which do not demand an active coping with conditions. For deliverance by means of rites and cults, it substituted deliverance through reason." Philosophical reason did not directly confront human experience in an effort to clarify it: experience was not to be trusted. Reason sought a higher reality which, if discovered, would clarify the totality of existence. The acceptance of a two-vision world defined philosophy's task and determined its future. The discipline was to concern itself with the "disclosure of the Real in itself, of Being in and of itself." It became preoccupied "with a higher and more ultimate form of Being than that with which the sciences of nature are concerned."[4]

Through centuries of philosophical thinking since antiquity, man has continued to be wary of the changing and problematic. Like other men, philosophers have been "impatient with doubt and suspense" and have scurried away from it.[5] Necessity and science have drawn philosophers closer to humanistic pursuits, but too frequently they have taken pains not to confront the totality of human experience. Armed with a talent for selective perception, philosophers have allowed themselves to dissect experience, cutting away and discarding the uncertain while maintaining that which appears to be stable. For example, idealism ignored the actual process of thought which renders the world meaningful through interaction and chose to equate thought with 'reality' itself. By ignoring the ways in which man and world interact and the process through which meaning is formed, idealism converted thought into "an act of original and final creation." By doing so, it freed man from the precarious aspects of experience. The mind became the sole constituent within the idealistic framework: the world existed only for the convenience of consciousness. Dewey explained that idealism "fails to take into account the specified or concrete character of the uncertain situation in which thought occurs: it fails to note the empirically concrete nature of subject-matter, arts, and tools by which determination and consistency are reached."[6]

To take another example, realism holds that the mind is a passive agent in experience, that objects of knowledge are impressed upon the mind but are not affected by it. This model of the mind relieves consciousness of its constitutive powers and redefines conscious action as a mechanical apparatus, programmed to respond in predictable fashion to external, inherently meaningful, stimuli. According to Dewey:

> Realists have constantly held that the traits which are characteristic of thinking, namely, uncertainty, ambiguity, alternatives, inquiring, search, selection, experimental reshaping of external conditions, do not possess the same existential character as do the objects of valid knowledge. They have denied that these traits are evidential of the character of the world within which thinking occurs. They have not . . . asserted that these traits are mere appearances; but they have often asserted and implied that such things are only personal or psychological in contrast with a world of objective nature.[7]

We need not trace in detail the myriad consequences of dualistic thinking on Western philosophy. That ground has been well plowed by others.[8] The point to be emphasized is that dualism separated such things as mind and matter, man and nature, and emotion and intellect, making it nearly impossible to examine human experience in an organismic, holistic way.

With mind and matter depicted as radically different in character, it becomes a bewildering problem to explain their relationship. Philosophers through the ages have asked, How is it that the mind can come to know the world in which it is placed? What relationship exists between ideas and the outer world, between precepts and concepts? Some philosophers have answered the question by eradicating it. Minds, they say, do not know the world because they cannot; perceptions are illusions. Others defined 'knowing' as a process of divine imprinting, a gift of God that has nothing in common with the character of the objective world.

The advent of modern science supplied philosophers, and eventually social scientists, with a mechanistic model of the mind which reduced perception to a mechanical act. It is this image which social science has inherited and which has been kept alive by behaviorists in psychology and by structural functionalists in sociology.

The model of mechanomorphic man depicts human life as devoid of ambiguity. The stark, bloodless metaphor of humming machinery defines existence through the action and reaction (stimulus-response) calculations of Newtonian physics. The mind, said Isaiah Berlin, has been treated at least since Locke and his fellow empiricists "as if it were a box containing mental equivalents of the Newtonian particles." Ideas and perceptions, as defined by this model of mind, originate in an external world and drop "into the mind like so many grains of sand inside an hourglass."[9]

Science had clarified the world for Locke, Hume, and their French followers. As Isaiah Berlin explained, they believed "what science had achieved in the sphere of the material world [could also be achieved] in the sphere of the mind and . . . in the realm of social and political relations." The inner worlds of thought and emotion could be measured and manipulated in the same way as objects of the outer world. "Men were objects in nature no less than trees and stones; their interaction could be studied as that of atoms or plants. Once the laws governing human behavior were discovered and incorporated in a science of rational sociology, analogous to physics or zoology, men's real wishes could be investigated . . . and satisfied. . . . The ideal of creating a wholly just, wholly virtuous, wholly satisfied society was therefore no longer utopian."[10] Certainty was at last within man's grasp.

Such a view is dangerous. It reduces the mind to the image of a machine and the entire individual sometimes disappears from sight. How like the views of many present-day social scientists are the words of Comte's contemporary Maine de Biran.

Not the human mind, not the individual understanding are the true subjects of the notions and verities of human existence. Society, however, gifted with a kind of collective mind, different from the individual's, is imbued with such knowledge. The individual, the human being is nothing; society alone exists. . . .

It alone has reality, while individuals are only phenomena. . . . If this is true, all philosophy of the past was wrong. One must recognize the failure of the science of the intellectual and moral man, one must admit the failure of psychology which has its basis in the primitive fact of conscience.[11]

However great the spread of time between early man's quest for certainty and the beginning work of the American behaviorists, they shared the same goal, namely, the annihilation of ambiguity and the discovery of a world of perfect calculability. John Watson, one of the founders of the behaviorist school of psychology, envisioned a new age of social engineering which studied behavior by one "rule or measuring rod." Confronted with any human activity he would ask, "Can I describe this bit of behavior I see in terms of 'stimulus and response'?"[12] Armed with this outlook, an aristocracy of psychologists was to "finally" rid the world of its uncertain future. They would succeed, they promised, where other hopeful Utopians had failed. Said Watson:

> If one were to characterize social experimentation in general during the past 2,000 years one would have to call it precipitous, infantile, unplanned, and say that when planned it is always in the interests of some nation, political group, sect or individual, *rather than under the guidance of social scientists*. . . . Never, except possibly at certain periods of Grecian history, have we had even an educated ruling class. Our own country today is one of the worst offenders in history. [Italics added.][13]

If a behaviorist could control the environment, Watson claimed, he could train a normal infant "to become any type of specialist . . . doctor, lawyer, artist, merchant-chief and, yes, even beggar-man and thief." Behaviorism would give man freedom, not "freedom of the libertine, but behavioristic freedom—a freedom which we cannot even picture in words, so little do we know of it."[14] This freedom from the ravages of uncertainty offered a promised land of peace. By mechanomorphicizing man, the behaviorist believed he had rendered the world predictable and thus controllable. This view of man and the future had appeal. As one historian of American psychology has put it, behaviorism has "an optimistic faith in the capacity of science to take charge of human affairs. [It offered] young men and women of the time a new . . . hope when the old guides had become hopelessly discredited in their eyes. It was a religion to take the place of religion."[15]

Like so many before, it was a religion which deprived man of the creative force of his intelligence. By degrading human activity to the status of a simple response to outside stimuli, man was left without internal initiative, without the power to create meaning. Behaviorists have little use for the concept of meaning. As Watson explained, behaviorists don't "believe the word is needed or that it is useful except as a literary expression."[16] Such a position deprives man of striving and purpose and indeed of consciousness itself. Watson disciple Z. Y. Kuo simply said of this criticism that "the concept of purpose is a lazy substitute for . . . careful and detailed analysis. . . . With better understanding of the . . . elementary stimuli and the stimulus pattern . . . the concept of purpose of whatever form will eventually disappear. . . . The duty of a behaviorist is to describe behavior in exactly the same way as the physicist describes the movement of a machine. . . . This human machine behaves in a certain way because environmental stimulation has forced him to do so."[17]

The long history of thought which expelled intelligent man from the universe, or reduced him to a mechanism capable only of response, is matched by a similar effort to bring him back into a meaningful union with nature. Some philosophers fled materialism only to retreat into idealism. Others struggled for a synthesis between man and world which recognized the full character of each. Their synthesis would preserve man's creative capacity to revolt—what Max Scheler recognized as the power to detach oneself from events, to say no to portions of one's world.[18] Such a view of man-in-the-world would recognize the power and significance of forces external to man, but at the same time be cognizant of possible human skepticism, man's significant ability to question taken-for-granted portions of his environment.

If science did not inform man of his capacity for revolt, then common sense did. Such men as Vico, James, and later Husserl, Mead, and Dewey, to name an important few, refused to commit an act of bad faith by denying man his capacity for freedom. They sought synthesis where others had contented themselves with half truths. Returning to experience, they explained man's existence on his own terms rather than on the basis of models adapted from economics, physics, or metaphysics. They were not convinced that the study of man necessitated a choice between the "interior" human spirit and the "exterior" world of things. Such clear categories do not exist in lived experience. Only if we view selected portions of experience can we talk of man as separate from the world of his experience.

It is possible and perhaps even necessary for philosophical work to break down experience into components. But such an exercise must be done consciously, carefully, and for analytical purposes only. If we view experience solely as an effort to distinguish a stimulus from a response, we will usually find what we seek: such outcomes are predetermined from the start. But we will find pure categories only in abstraction and not in reality. Human experience is not so easily classifiable.

The behaviorist's model of man views experience only in terms of its behavioral outcomes. It ignores purposeful efforts and innovation. This bifurcated stimulus-response vision of experience is deemed essential by such behaviorists as B. F. Skinner, who contends, "The hypothesis that man is not free is essential to the application of scientific method to the study of human behavior."[19] To deal with the concept of freedom in purely scientific terms presents problems: science seeks causality and is incapable of proving that any action originates in total freedom.[20] Yet it is quite another thing to assume there are no problems at all—only myths of freedom and dignity which we must not confront but rather move beyond. Skinner limits the problem of human behavior for the convenience of a methodology inherited from the natural sciences. As Whitehead points out: "You cannot limit a problem by reason of a method of attack. The problem is to understand the operations of an animal body. There is clear evidence that certain operations of certain animal bodies depend upon the foresight of an end and the purpose to attain it. It is no solution of the problem to ignore this evidence because other operations have been explained in terms of physical and chemical laws."[21]

If we view experience holistically, as it is lived, we discover its components. The experience, the experiencing act, the experienced entity, the background against which that entity stands out—all are held together in organic unity through the configuration of meaning. Only by viewing experience in its entirety do we come to understand the significance of meaning in human activity. As Ernest Becker has described it:

> Meaning is the great truth about human nature. Everything that lives, lives by drawing together strands of experience as a basis for action; to live is to act, to move forward into the world

of experience. Meaning . . . is the drawing together of aspects of experience for action and well-being. Meaning is the relationship between parts of experience.[22]

The discovery (and continual rediscovery) of meaning in experience quickly exposes the inadequacy of the mechanomorphic model of man. Man's capacity to grasp and create meaning makes him neither master nor slave of his world. It divulges the ways he is part of, and interacts with, nature. The stimulus-response model of man may free us at least temporarily from the nagging ambiguities of life, but it offers no explanation for man's being-in-the-world. By failing to acknowledge the purposeful powers of creative intelligence, it enslaves man to given and fixed ends of external forces. Dewey offers another angle of vision, and it is worthwhile to quote him at length:

> The pragmatic theory of intelligence means that the function of mind is to project new and more complex ends—to free experience from routine and from caprice. . . . Action restricted to given and fixed ends may attain great technical efficiency; but efficiency is the only quality to which it can lay claim. Such action is mechanical (or becomes so), no matter what the scope of the performed end. . . . But the doctrine that intelligence develops within the sphere of action for the sake of possibilities not yet given is the opposite of a doctrine of mechanistic efficiency. Intelligence *as* intelligence is inherently forward looking; *only by ignoring its primary function does it become a mere means for an end already given.* A pragmatic intelligence is a creative intelligence, not a routine mechanic. [Italics added.][23]

Of course it is possible to study human behavior without considering the components of creative intelligence. Traffic patterns, for example, may be viewed in strict stimulus-response terms, and much may be learned through such a study. We would see that red lights correlate highly with halted traffic, and road signs influence driving behavior. We would not learn why these systems "work." We would not understand the process through which they derive meaning. And we would never be able to grasp why some people are influenced by red lights and road signs and others are not. Without consulting the intentions of individual drivers, the traffic patterns of a big city are little more than a meaningless, random milling of automobiles. And so it is with all human behavior. To neglect the intention of the behaver is to lose the significance of his behavior.

We cannot study human behavior as we would, for example, the movement of planets. The movements of Venus against a darkened sky can be deciphered mathematically. But to the degree that man is capable of meaning, his actions are not revealed by simply calculating the forces affecting him. The essential difference is that these forces have meaning for the human subject of our study, whereas the forces which influence Venus have no meaning for the planet. The movement of Venus, for example, would not be affected by a terrestrial stop sign placed beside its path in space.[24]

Both man and his behavior are the subject matter of the social scientist, whose first duties are to respect his subject matter, to greet it on its own terms, and to be open to its inherent possibilities. The ensuing study attempts to greet human behavior holistically and on its own terms. It tries to recognize the essential nature of uncertainty rather than fleeing from it, and to discover its rightful place in experience. Rather than denying the existence of meaning, spontaneity, and purposeful human action, it will embrace them as essential to an explanation of experience. This will not be an excursion into the behavioral sciences but an attempt to get at prior issues regarding human conduct. In that sense, this study is a philosophical attempt at metatheory for the social sciences, setting down in concise terms the genesis and organization of human experience.

No longer can we afford the myopic view of experience held presently by many social scientists. Cramming our view of experience (the basis for how we view ourselves) into prefabricated and long-outmoded theoretical frames is a dangerous undertaking. Our recent historical agonies are ugly testimony to our need to better understand and intelligently confront the actualities of human existence. On the eve of World War I, Dewey wrote that "all peoples at all times have been narrowly realistic in practice and have then employed idealization to cover up in sentiment and theory their brutalities. But never, perhaps, has the tendency been so dangerous and so tempting as with ourselves."[25] Such a sentiment is even more urgent a half-century later. Social science theories will have to return to lived experience and be consistent with what is found there.

Guiding the following exploration will be the works of two philosophers. Although very different in their backgrounds and approaches to philosophy, they had a similar passion for understanding human experience in its rich totality. The first of these is John Dewey, America's most eminent philosopher during the first half of this century. The second, Alfred Schutz, was European born. Although Schutz gained recognition among philosophers and sociologists, he remains largely unknown by persons outside these fields. For that reason, some space will be given to an examination of his philosophical career.

An examination of experience borrowing unabashedly from both phenomenology and pragmatism not only examines the genesis and organization of human experience but serves a larger cause. Richard Bernstein has identified this in the last chapter of his book-length study of Dewey.

> There is also a good deal in common between Dewey and phenomenology, especially in its recent developments. For this movement, too, has rebelled against the mind-body dualism implicit in the Cartesian tradition of modern philosophy. As the works of the phenomenologists are being translated into English, it becomes increasingly evident that phenomenologists, like Dewey, seek to elaborate a rich theory of experience that escapes the dilemmas of rigid dualism and dichotomies. . . . It is too simple and misleading to declare that "they" are both saying the same thing. But there is a common platform on which there can be fruitful dialogue between Dewey and phenomenology, a dialogue that could enrich both phenomenology and the pragmatic tradition.[26]

Such a dialogue was slow in developing, but it is under way. This study hopes to add to that exchange.

2. Schutz and Dewey on the Problem of Relevance

THE PHILOSOPHICAL WORK
OF ALFRED SCHUTZ

Aʟꜰʀᴇᴅ Sᴄʜᴜᴛᴢ was in Paris on business when the Nazis invaded Austria in 1938. Rather than return to Vienna, where he was born 13 April 1899, he arranged for his family to join him in France. On 14 July 1939, he embarked with his wife and children for the United States to renew a banking career begun in his Austrian homeland.

Schutz brought with him to America a remarkably wide range of interests and talents which had begun to emerge years before in Vienna. He graduated from Esterhazy Gymnasium at 17, completing a curriculum which included eight years of Latin and Greek. A year of military service during World War I brought him decorations for bravery on the Italian front. Returning home after the war, he en-rolled at the University of Vienna, in two-and-one-half years completing a four-year course of study leading to a Doctorate in Law. His wide-ranging interests brought him into the university classes of such notables as Hans Kelsen (law), Ludwig von Mises (economics), Friedrick von Wieser and Othmar Spann (sociology).[1] Although Schutz was to maintain deep interests in, and talents for, widely diversified areas of study, he never treated them in departmentalized fashion. He was able to bring his interests together—for example, his knowledge of law, philosophy, and music—to further his work in theoretical sociology. He possessed one of those rare, world-spanning, thoroughly original minds, which was able to discover unity where others found only discord.

This talent for unification was clearly evident in Schutz's first book and the only one published during his lifetime—*Phenomenology of the Social World*. The book grew out of years of studying Max Weber and the realization that Weber neglected critically important areas, although he had made an invaluable contribution to sociology. Schutz says in the book's introduction, "Above all, Weber's central concept of subjective meaning calls for a thoroughgoing analysis. As

11

Weber left this concept it was little more than a heading for a number of important problems which he did not examine in detail, even though they were hardly foreign to him." Schutz traced Weber's thoughts back to their epistemological foundations and then proceeded to extend his argument by exploring what Schutz called "the fundamental facts of conscious life."[2] He confronted and tried to solve the problem of meaning and its connection with human action which existed in, but was not solved by, Weber's work. His task was to build a philosophical fundament on which Weber's interpretive sociology could be erected.

Schutz approached this task through the use of Bergsonian and especially Husserlian categories. Some years earlier, he had read Husserl's *Logical Investigations* with interest and a sense of its importance but without great enthusiasm. Only later, after reading for the first time Husserl's *Phenomenology of Internal Time-Consciousness*, was he "catapulted into phenomenology."[3] In bringing together the perspectives of Weber and Husserl, he was able to open whole new areas for sociological study, notably the social construction of reality.

His *Phenomenology of the Social World* was published in 1932 by Julius Springer. Although the agonies of the impending war no doubt curtailed the influence of the book, it nevertheless found its way into the thinking of some of Europe's most astute scholars. For example, references to this book can be found in the writings of Jose Ortega y Gasset, Raymond Aron, Felix Kaufmann, and Ludwig von Mises.[4] The significance of Schutz's work was quickly recognized by Edmund Husserl, who wrote Schutz shortly after the book's publication. "I am anxious to meet such a serious and thorough phenomenologist. [You are] one of the few who have penetrated to the core of the meaning of my life's work, access to which is unfortunately so difficult, and who promises to continue it as representative of the genuine *philosophia perennis*, which alone can be the future of philosophy."[5] Shortly thereafter, Schutz traveled to meet Husserl and was asked to become his assistant. Schutz was unable to accept the offer but kept in close contact with Husserl through frequent visits and lengthy correspondence until Husserl's death in 1938.

Although Schutz was influenced profoundly by Husserl's work, it would be wrong to view him as a mere disciple of Husserlian phenomenology. He was a 'careful critic of Husserl and in some areas was boldly original. In some respects, said Thomas Luckmann,

Schutz's writings can be viewed as "an impressive continuation of the central concerns" of both Husserl and Weber. Nevertheless, he was to make significant contributions of his own to philosophy and the social sciences. As Luckmann stated the case, "There can be no doubt that Schutz's orginal thinking and systematic investigations led him into new territory, where neither Husserl, whose acquaintance with the social sciences did not match his knowledge of the physical sciences (and his mastery of mathematics and logic), nor Weber, whose thinking never entirely dissociated itself from conventional Neo-Kantian philosophical premises, might have wanted to follow him."[6]

More than any other phenomenologist to date, Schutz was able to wed the social sciences to philosophy where, after all, they had originated. He did not accomplish this merely by bringing a few philosophical ideas to sociology or simply by looking at the discipline from a philosophical point of view. "To understand Schutz's sociology," wrote Maurice Natanson, "it is imperative to realize that he was not influenced by philosophy; he was a philosopher! He was not influenced by phenomenology; he was a phenomenologist!" What makes Schutz's work significant is not his application of philosophy to sociology, but his uniting these fields in perspective and purpose. Natanson makes the point with characteristic eloquence. Schutz was able to demonstrate that "at their theoretical fundament, sociology and philosophy are one."[7] In addition to being a philosopher, sociologist, and student of law, Schutz was a full-time banker. His accomplishments in the former fields are made even more remarkable when it is realized that of necessity his intellectual work was done on a part-time basis.

These were the talents, interests and accomplishments which Schutz possessed when he arrived in New York at the age of 40. The intellectual climate he was to find in America was very different from the one he left behind in Europe. Phenomenology was foreign to Americans and viewed with some suspicion. It is true that phenomenology had an American anchorage in the most original thoughts of William James. There is a strand woven through his writings, particularly in his monumental *Principles of Psychology*, which is clearly phenomenological. It was this strand which Husserl credited with leading him out of the wilderness of psychologism (the view that psychology was the ultimate discipline), where so many thinkers had become lost.[8] But if phenomenology had American roots, it bore no fruit in this country and Schutz was not to find a ready audience for his ideas. He was going to have to start again, this time at the very beginning, by introducing phenomenology to a philosophic community which had no interest in, and in some cases only hostility toward, its perspectives. Schutz began an article published in *Social Research* in 1945 by saying:

> An unsigned booknote in an issue of the *American Sociological Review*, discussing phenomenological literature, regrets that these writings are almost inaccessible even to many philosophers, to say nothing of social scientists. "We must apparently wait for popularized interpretations before much can be said about the relations of phenomenology and the social sciences." Unfortunately, this description of the situation is not exaggerated. So far, social scientists have not found an adequate approach to the phenomenological movement initiated by the basic writings of Edmund Husserl in the first three decades of our century. In certain quarters the phenomenologist is held to be a kind of crystal gazer, a metaphysician or ontologist in the deprecatory sense of the words, at any rate a fellow who spurns all empirical facts and the more or less established scientific methods devised to collect and interpret them. Others, who are better informed, feel that phenomenology may have a certain significance for the social sciences, but they regard the phenomenologists as an esoteric group whose language is not understandable to an outsider and is not worth bothering with. A third group has formed a vague and mostly erroneous idea of what phenomenology means, on the basis of some of the slogans used by authors who merely pretend to be phenomenologists, without using Husserl's method (such as Theodor Litt) or used by phenomenologists (such as Max Scheler) in non-phenomenological writings dealing with the social sciences.[9]

This state of affairs must have been terribly frustrating for a man who had already made a significant contribution to phenomenology. Not only did he have to face the problems of being an immigrant in a strange land, but he had to live with the realization that he was deprived of an audience for his ideas. Similar conditions led phenomenologist Aron Gurwitsch, who arrived on American shores in 1940, to describe his first two decades in the United States as "climbing the mountain of cotton."[10] These conditions were even more prevalent in sociology. Philosophy itself—let alone an esoteric, European-based philosophy—was viewed by many as simply irrelevant.

Schutz's brand of sociology was not going to be understood. A humorous example of this situation typifies it. During Schutz's first professional meeting of sociologists, a friend introduced him to a colleague, saying, "Dr. Schutz is also a sociologist." "Oh," came the reply, "urban or rural?"[11] At least in America, Schutz was beginning in a field where there were no categories for him. Alfred Schutz was, in the most pregnant sense of the word, a stranger.

There can be little doubt that Schutz's penetrating article, "The Stranger," which was published a few years after his arrival in New York, was at least partly an intellectual exploration of his own, early experience in the United States. "The stranger," he wrote, "has to face the fact that he lacks any status as a member of the social group he is about to join and is therefore unable to get a starting-point [from which] to take his bearings. He finds himself a border case outside the territory covered by the scheme of orientation current within the group. He is, therefore, no longer permitted to consider himself as the center of his social environment, and this fact causes . . . a dislocation of his contour lines of relevance."[12]

An immigrant leaves behind much more than his past, his belongings, and his culture when he enters a new and different land. There is the profound possibility that he leaves behind portions of himself as well. Portions of being which receive no recognition in the new setting, or are defined differently therein, literally can be detached from an individual to wither without social sustenance. This might have happened to Schutz had he not been so firmly convinced of the value of phenomenology. He re-entered the banking profession on arrival in New York, working primarily on questions of law and international finance. His success in that field, coupled with the slim chance that phenomenology would gain recognition in the United States, might have convinced a lesser man to allow his philosophical interests to be dissolved slowly by the burdens of everyday life. It is to Schutz's credit, and to the benefit of American social science, that philosophy and sociology remained central in his mind. The fact that he carried on two professions simultaneously and with such success in a foreign land makes his contributions to phenomenology all the more remarkable. Husserl admiringly described Schutz to Aron Gurwitsch as "a bank executive by day and a phenomenologist by night."[13] Natanson said of this union that it was "not only understandable but even necessary—as remarkable yet as natural as the combination of insurance and poetry in the life of Wallace Stevens."[14]

The ensuing study will not be able to do justice to the strength and character of Schutz. Such a task is better suited to those who worked with him and studied under his direction. It may not be inappropriate to quote H. L. van Breda's comments from the preface to the first volume of Schutz's collected works. Van Breda gives us the key to understanding the breadth of Schutz's life and work, namely, his passion to understand man.

> I would like to speak of the man, to evoke the acumen of his mind, his penetrating irony, his serenity and courage in exile, the wide range of his interests, the gift of youthfulness and sympathetic understanding which enabled him to assimilate successfully a new culture at the age of forty and to become accomplished in it. Fearing to say too little and to say it ineptly, I limit myself to recalling his unceasing passion to understand man. Schutz was a philosopher, a psychologist, a sociologist, a musicologist: all of these approaches served that passion.[15]

Many of the qualities of which van Breda speaks, as well as something of the problems Schutz faced as a phenomenologist in American social science, converge in the history of the first writing Schutz undertook for an American audience. On arriving in this country, Schutz began to read voraciously the works of American philosophers and social scientists. He was already familiar with Talcott Parsons, a rising star in American sociology. Parsons's book, *Structures of Social Action*, had been published in 1937, and Schutz had read it before he left Europe. He had been asked to write a lengthy review of the book for the English journal *Economica*, which he completed in the summer of 1939. Shortly after arriving in America, he met Parsons, whose work had not received much attention in Europe and who looked forward to what such an eminent European sociologist-philosopher as Schutz would have to say about it. Schutz decided to send him a copy of the 74-page, essay-length review, "The Social World and Theory of Social Action," before submitting it to *Economica*.

Parsons's response to the essay convinced Schutz that his criticism of the structural functionalist school of sociology was not going to be understood by a public unacquainted with the phenomenological perspective. Because misunderstanding was sure to follow, and because this misunderstanding would make impossible the scholarly debate he had hoped his manuscript would precipitate, Schutz decided against its publication. However, this decision was not a strategic move by a man with an eye on his career. It was a move by a man of scholarly instincts who would not level an attack on a school of thought, if the proponents of that school were unable to grasp the substance of his criticism. This action stemmed from that capacity for "sympathetic understanding" of which van Breda spoke.

Even when phenomenology was gaining recognition in later years (largely as the result of Schutz's efforts), Schutz refrained from publishing his critique of Parsons. The manuscript remained unpublished until after his death when a portion of it, which dealt only with phenomenology, was excerpted and published in *Social Research*.[16] The remainder of the paper has been kept out of print by Mrs. Schutz, who only recently consented to publication after receiving assurances from Parsons that he approves of the work finally coming before the public.

Shortly after arriving in New York, Schutz joined Alvin Johnson's University in Exile, later to become the graduate faculty of the New School for Social Research. After a day in the business world, Schutz conducted evening classes in philosophy and the social sciences. Schutz hoped that the philosophy department of the New School would some day become the American center for phenomenological studies. He kept in close contact with philosophers of a phenomenological persuasion—Dorion Cairns, Aron Gurwitsch, and Marvin Farber, to name a few—and worked to bring some of these men to the New School.[17] Farber and Schutz organized the International Phenomenological Society in 1941, and Schutz became a member of the board of editors for its journal, *Philosophy and Phenomenological Research*.

Through his writing and teaching in the years that followed, Schutz worked to bring phenomenology before the American philosophical community for a fair hearing. He published thirty-one articles during his career, most of them in English. By keeping his audience carefully in mind, Schutz was able to introduce phenomenology while simultaneously exploring new ground. He was able to enrich his perspectives by reading widely and was especially interested in such American pragmatists as William James, Alfred North Whitehead, John Dewey, G. H. Mead, Charles Peirce, and C. I. Lewis. Sociologists of the Chicago school (notably Charles Cooley and W. I. Thomas), who had themselves been deeply influenced by the pragmatism of Dewey and Mead, also were read carefully by Schutz. Maurice Natanson, his student and trusted friend, described Schutz's method of study.

"Schutz's procedure in studying a new and major thinker was to immerse himself thoroughly in his works, to write notes of considerable length about them, and to try to master the author in the most painstaking manner."[18]

Schutz was never narrow. He was always willing to entertain new ideas and to make the effort necessary to understand a philosopher on his own terms. He was, as Richard Zaner has said, "tolerant and open in the finest philosophical tradition."[19] This was so characteristic of Schutz that it will be important to keep it in mind as this study proceeds. It is worth underlining the point with one more reference, this time from Ilse Schutz, who played an important role in the intellectual life of her husband. "My husband's approach to and his interest in everything connected even remotely with his own work and thoughts was a very broad and deep and open one and he studied Whitehead just as intensely as Max Weber or Husserl."[20]

Schutz's influence as a teacher will no doubt be the subject of a major study in years to come. The loyalty of his students and their deep affection for him are testimony to his talent. But beyond Schutz's personal contribution to the intellectual growth of his students, through them he also made a lasting contribution to philosophy and the social sciences. New perspectives have been introduced to sociology by Peter Berger, Thomas Luckmann, and Helmut Wagner. The phenomenological perspective is now a major force in sociology, where not long ago structural functionalism reigned supreme and uncontested. The works of Richard Zaner and Maurice Natanson are making an impact in American philosophy, where phenomenology is a relatively new but powerful force. The fact that these men—all students of Schutz—have found a willing if not always ready (in the sense of being informed) audience for their ideas is due, in large part, to the groundwork laid by Alfred Schutz.

Those who give birth to ideas, like those who give birth to children, inevitably see their offspring develop lives of their own over which parents have little control. Inevitably it must be so with the pioneering works of Schutz. The phenomenological perspective is so complex and in many respects so rich, that phenomenological social science could encounter two dangers in the future. One—perhaps the more unlikely given the quality of Schutz's first generation of students —is that his followers will miss in their enthusiasm the openness with which Schutz dealt with problems of philosophy. Were that to occur, Schutzian scholars might begin to concern themselves more with questions of "purity"—How closely does an idea replicate Schutz's thought?—than with continuing or extending his work. For such purists, merely suggesting the topic of this study would be anathema.

At the other end of the continuum, and perhaps even more damaging than the purist mentality, we can expect to find those who are inclined to use phenomenology as a metaphor for simplistic subjectivity. This perspective is perhaps most alive in introspectionist psychology at present, but it does have representatives in sociology as well.[21] The danger is that phenomenology will suffer in sociology the same problems that pragmatism suffered in education; namely, that many who will call themselves phenomenologists will remain blissfully ignorant of what phenomenology is about or of what the leading phenomenologists have said.

As is so often the case with diametrically opposite dangers, these two perspectives are likely to feed on each other. Should slipshod phenomenology prevail, it likely would be met by a counter-offensive of puritanism. The soft-mindedness of the ignorant and the narrow-mindedness of the purist would then combine to halt the wide-ranging and open-minded dialogue which Schutz began with the other schools of American philosophy and social sciences. This study is dedicated to continuing this dialogue and to recognizing Schutz's ability to seek unity without forcing it.

REFLECTIONS ON THE PROBLEM OF RELEVANCE AND OTHER WRITINGS BY ALFRED SCHUTZ

At many points in his work, Schutz made passing reference to the question of relevance, usually saying it was a topic of major importance, worthy of lengthy exploration, but beyond the scope of his present study. By "relevance," Schutz meant the process by which objects come to man's attention, the process which determines what is and what is not pertinent to the situation at hand. This line of inquiry submerges the *what* of consciousness and digs at the *why* it (rather than something else) is found within attention. "Let us make clear what is meant by 'relevance'," said Schutz.

> I am, for instance, with the natural attitude, passionately interested in the results of my action and especially in the question whether my anticipations will stand the practical test. As we have seen before, all anticipations and plans refer to previous experiences now at hand, which enable me to weigh my chances.

But that is only half the story. *What I* am anticipating is one thing, the other, *why* I anticipate certain occurrences at all. What may happen under certain conditions and circumstances is one thing, the other, why I am interested in these happenings and why I should passionately await the outcome of my prophecies. It is only the first part of these dichotomies which is answered by reference to the stock of experiences at hand as the sediment of previous experiences. It is the second part of these dichotomies which refers to the system of relevances by which man within his natural attitude in daily life is guided. [Schutz's italics.][22]

The problem of relevance was of more than peripheral interest for Schutz: it struck at the core concern of his life work. "It might be said," writes Maurice Natanson, "that the philosophy of Alfred Schutz articulates a single intuition, the discovery in the full depth of the presuppositions, structure and signification of the commonsense world." Despite their remarkable breadth, all Schutz's scholarly writings cohere to this driving interest and central theme. This was the *"fil conducteur* of his intellectual life, . . . a concern for the meaningful structure of the world of daily life, the everyday working world into which each of us is born, within whose limits our existence unfolds, and which we transcend completely only in death."[23] Until the problem of relevance is confronted directly, the full significance of the commonsense world must remain adumbrated.

An understanding of man in mundane life, Schutz contended, was possible only through a bold exploration of the structures, processes, and organization of human experience. It would not be achieved merely by tracing habitual human behavior as it evolves in already meaningful situations. It was to be grasped fully only when the constitution of meaning itself was explored. It would not be understood merely by cataloguing and analyzing conscious action but would be explained fully only when the precognitive elements which fund all conscious action could be approached and clarified. These are the domains of the problem of relevance. Here are found the questions dealing with how man is motivated to action: What accounts for the selectivity of consciousness and the organization of experience? Why are *these* things rather than others the topic of man's attention? What is the genesis of inquiry? How are problematic situations first constituted and then interpreted? and What accounts for man's ability to hypothesize and then test solutions to his problems at hand? These are vast questions. It is not surprising that Schutz chose to put off dealing with them fully until his schedule permitted time for their exhaustive exploration.

Schutz had realized the critical importance of the problem of relevance in his earliest writings. The next to the last page of his first book, *Phenomenology of the Social World*, contains this observation: "A second group of problems reaches far beyond the boundaries of the subject matter of the social sciences. It is the whole *problem of relevance*, which has kept cropping up again and again in the present study. The definitive clarification of this problem will be possible only through an over-all phenomenological analysis, which nevertheless can be begun within the field of the social sciences." (Schutz's italics.) [24]

In the years that followed, Schutz approached these problems again and again, dealing with parts of them in articles but always contemplating and working toward their final clarification in a major, book-length study. During occasional vacation trips to Colorado and at night and on weekends, Schutz found time to begin dealing in systematic fashion with the problem of relevance. Between August 1947 and August 1951, he worked on a manuscript to be titled "The World Taken-for-Granted: Toward a Phenomenology of the Natural Attitude." It was to be a five-part study, the first portion of which was to deal with relevance. The project was never completed, but its first section, although itself not complete, was close enough to publishable form to deserve printing. The manuscript was found among Schutz's papers after his death. Ilse Schutz, together with Thomas Luckmann and Richard Zaner, decided that although Schutz did not intend publication as it stood, it should nevertheless be made available to students of phenomenology in book form. Zaner undertook the job of editing the book, and it was published in 1970 under the title *Reflections on the Problems of Relevance*. "Even though the study was conceived as only the first of five parts," wrote Zaner in the book's introduction, "I believe it can and does stand alone as a separate piece, important in its own right. And while some of the issues with which it is concerned are treated elsewhere in his writings, Schutz's analysis of them here is much more detailed and, in any event, of sufficient strength and inherent value to merit separate publication." [25]

In a letter to Zaner, Ilse Schutz described the setting in which her husband wrote the major portions of *Reflections on the Problems of Relevance*.

We were in Colorado. He went every morning on a long walk
which led to a beautiful spot surrounded by mountains and
meadows. It was a kind of outdoor Lutheran church and a
meeting-ground for its members and there were tables and
benches. He loved this place dearly and it provided an ideal
place for meditating and writing. And there it was where the
Reflections on Relevance came into being.[26]

Perhaps because his schedule so limited the time he had available
for scholarly work, Schutz had to direct all of his writings toward a
much larger project—*Structures of the Life-World*—the publication
of which was to be the zenith of his life's work. All of his writing was
done with that book clearly in mind. Discussing *Reflections on the
Problems of Relevance* in this context, Ilse Schutz stated that "all his
papers were destined to be part of his planned book. And the *Relevance* manuscript even more so."[27]

The writing and publication of *Structures of the Life-World* was
of increasing concern to Schutz during the 1950s. He completed out-
lines for the book and was able to free himself of some other obliga-
tions in order to devote more time to writing. This work was not completed at the time of his death but was in sufficiently clear form to
allow Thomas Luckmann to undertake the monumental task of completing it. The first of two volumes of this study is in print at the time
of this writing. It is clearly a book of co-authorship, but Luckmann
has been able to remain remarkably true to Schutz's work and the
book is invaluable to those interested in pursuing Schutz's thoughts.
Although it deals centrally with the theory of relevance, it does not
alter significantly what Schutz sets forth in the *Reflections* book. It
exceeds the accomplishments of the latter book by integrating the
theory of relevance within the full context of Schutz's phenomenological explanation of the *Lebenswelt* and his theory of the social world.

Shortly before his death, Schutz asked Maurice Natanson to undertake the editing of his scattered writings. The plan was for Natanson
to eliminate the repetition found in Schutz's many papers, cross-
reference and index the work, make editorial changes and clarifica-
tions where necessary, and write a general introduction to the collected papers. All this was to be done with Schutz overseeing the
project. He died, however, before he could approve Natanson's plan,
and Natanson, together with Mrs. Schutz, decided to publish the collected papers with a minimum of editorial alteration. All but a few of

Schutz's writings are now available in three volumes published by Martinus Nijhoff, The Hague, Netherlands.[28]

MEANING, RELEVANCE, AND THE PRE-REFLECTIVE IN THE WRITING OF JOHN DEWEY

Pragmatism is America's only native philosophy, and John Dewey's seminal works stand at its center. His influence on the course of twentieth-century American intellectual thought has been dramatic and profound. The modern development of sociology, law, political and social theory, religion, and of course education has been nurtured and enriched by Dewey's contribution. "Further thought in America must go beyond Dewey," observed Robert Roth, "though it is difficult to see how it can avoid going through him."[29]

The meaning and significance of Dewey's thought, its influence and the controversies which accompanied it, as well as his intellectual career, need not be reviewed. These topics have been explored often, and books are readily available. Instead, we will deal in introductory fashion with one area of Dewey's work which has not received the attention it deserves, namely, his views on relevance and the pre-reflective workings of consciousness.

Relevance at its heart is a question of discrimination. As Schutz said, it is "the question of why these facts and precisely these are selected by thought from the totality of lived experience and regarded as relevant."[30] Before the turn of the century, Dewey was exploring just such ground. "Discrimination, not integration, is the real problem," he wrote. It is "the recognition of *this* object out of the multitude of possible objects, of just this bundle of vibrations out of all other bundles" which stands as the question to be answered. (Dewey's italics.)[31] Until the answer to this question is found, there is little hope of fully explicating human experience. The problem of relevance is, in fact, the problem of the genesis and organization of experience. To answer the question of relevance is to illuminate the genesis of inquiry, to clarify the meaning of consciousness, and to uncover the significance of the noncognitive domains of experience. The question is vitally important to philosophy. It probes the meaning of man's being in the world, the very possibility of his placement in reality.

Phenomenologists frequently contend that Dewey totally ignored the problem of relevance and other questions which originate in the pre-reflective realm. The assumption is that Dewey made careful and continued use of the scientific method but nevertheless neglected to investigate the presuppositions on which science itself rests. An example of this view is found in Maurice Natanson's article, "Being-in-Reality," published in *Philosophy and Phenomenological Research*, 1959.[32] Dewey has claimed that problems always arise within a context which is itself nonproblematic. Natanson believes that this observation is valid but of limited usefulness to philosophy. Such a position, Natanson contends, fails to investigate the unproblematic context itself. This, he says, is the more fundamental question for philosophy and one to be approached exclusively by phenomenology. It is worthwhile to quote Natanson at length on this point.

> To say, with Dewey, that every problem presupposes an unproblematic context within which, against which it arises, is to leave unexamined and unclarified the very meaning of "context." Whatever interpretation of "situation" Dewey presents is already founded on the assumption that we have, are *in*, or find or locate such a context. This assumption is proper to empirical science; in fact, it is its point of departure. But if part of the task of philosophy is to consider the foundational concepts and presuppositions of the sciences, it is necessary to start at the beginning and place in question what it means to take something as unproblematic. To do this is to shift from the natural standpoint to a reflective one; and to attempt to take the reflective standpoint itself as the object of scrutiny is to search for phenomenological roots.[33]

A theme of this study is to show that such an interpretation of Dewey's work is entirely too narrow, and that Dewey in fact did address himself to just the questions which Natanson tells us he failed to recognize. Dewey claimed of course that it is not necessary for us to examine context as we go about the "communications of every-day life." It can be "safely ignored," he said, because "it is irrevocably there. It is taken for granted, not denied, when it is passed over without notice." This simply says that *every* inquiry takes for granted *something*; no inquiry escapes the pervasive *fact* of context. But Dewey added emphatically that philosophy cannot afford likewise to ignore the significance and meaning of context. It is difficult to imagine how he could have made the point more forcefully. "I should venture to assert that the most pervasive fallacy of philosophic thinking goes back to [the] neglect of context." Such neglect, Dewey claimed, "is the greatest single disaster which philosophic thinking can incur."[34]

When Dewey first undertook to investigate logic, he began by pointing out that the organization of experience originates, not in the outcomes of science, but rather in the pre-reflective workings of intentional consciousness. It is here, Natanson believes, that we find "what it means to take something as unproblematic."[35] Significantly, it is here also that Dewey begins his first book-length inquiry into logic. In the introduction to *Essays in Experimental Logic*, Dewey bemoans the fact that the internal organization of experience "is thought of as the achieved outcome of a highly scientific knowledge, or the result of a transcendental rational synthesis, or as a fiction superinduced by association, upon elements each of which in its own right 'is a separate existence.' One advantage of an excursion by one who philosophizes upon knowledge into primary non-reflectional experience is that the excursion serves to remind him that every empirical situation has its own organization of a direct, non-logical character." A philosopher must continually remind himself that experience cannot be totally explained by its cognitive outcomes. "It is indispensable to note," said Dewey, "that . . . the intellectual element is set in a context which is non-cognitive and which holds within it in suspense a vast complex of other qualities and things. . . ."[36] Experience of whatever sort cannot be understood in totality without first bringing these elements, which exist only horizontally in the vaguest forms, into our reflective gaze for clarification. Only then will the full meaning of "context" be available to us. Only then will we be able to understand how situations are organized at the pre-reflective levels of consciousness.

Dewey's concern for the noncognitive stuff of experience (that which funds the object of attention with meaning) does not seem to differ from Natanson's contention that philosophy needs to explore the horizons of consciousness to discover how it is that man can *have* a world. Natanson has written: "When I move . . . from a 'this' to the vague form of 'world' surrounding and including that 'this,' I explore the phenomenological horizon of my immediate placement in reality." Natanson tells us that this shift of focus is accompanied by a radical departure from the natural attitude where the noncognitive is penumbral. It allows man to transpose "the naively experienced world into the intentional field of world-for-me." He turns his "glance from the 'real' object" which permeates experience "to the object as I take it, treat it, *interpret it* as real." (Italics added.)[37] In this way the object is seen as it is integrated pre-reflectively into the field of consciousness, that is, as it is known, meant, intended. In fact, to view an object as it is interpreted in consciousness is to view reflectively the workings of intentional consciousness itself, as it renders the world meaningful for men.

Dewey also believed that the objects of direct experience must be grasped at the level where they are funded with meaning. We will see this later in greater detail. Suffice it to say that Dewey did call for radical reflection and detachment from the natural attitude to examine just that area which Natanson believes he overlooks. "What other method of getting outside and beyond the things of direct experience is conceivable," asks Dewey, "save that of penetration to the conditions upon which they depend?"[38]

Natanson claims that Dewey is oblivious to such questions, because naturalism cannot work its way out of the natural attitude and take the stance of radical reflection. Thus, Natanson tells us that pragmatism is "founded on the assumption that the individual is, of course, already in the world when we *interrogate* him about his history and interests. The person is in the world in much the same way that marbles are in the bag, that a cat is in the house, that a teacher is in the classroom." This is not enough, says Natanson. "The full reality of the individual is surely not exhausted in statistics and the identity of the person demands an appreciation of *his* situation in the world. . . ."[39] Dewey is here accused of ignoring the full character of individual placement in the world.

Dewey was aware that the things of consciousness are *had* before they are perceived. He was also aware that an understanding of this "meaningful having" is only available through reflection. Only in reflection, Dewey tells us, can we grasp the "critical connections" of man and world and understand what it is to be an "organism *in* nature . . . not as marbles are in a box but as events are in history, in a moving, growing, never finished process." Dewey approached an understanding of man via his meaningful connection with the world, via the process of *having* his world. "Living," Dewey repeatedly reminded his readers, "is always an inclusive affair involving connection, interaction of what is within the organic body and what lies outside in space and time. . . ."[40] To grasp man as a conscious, living

creature, we must know how it is that he *has*, or in language closer
to phenomenology, how he *intends* a meaningful world.

Dewey's work refers repeatedly to these affairs. He attempts consistently to approach the intentionality of consciousness through a
contextual exploration of man's *having* of meaning. In this regard,
he would agree with Calvin Schrag, who said, "The question about
intentionality is at bottom a question about meaning."[41] Dewey
claims that a clear explanation of consciousness is "the open gate-
way into the fair fields of philosophy."[42] Certainly he was never
so narrow as to restrict philosophy to that small island of existence
where the scientific categories of truth and falsity are applicable.
He saw clearly that "a large part of our life is carried on in a realm
of meanings to which truth and falsity as such are irrelevant." The
proper task of philosophy, he said, is one of "liberating and clarifying meanings," not in the narrow sense of clarifying language (although this is important) but in the broadest sense of clarifying the
origin of meaning.[43] The deeper he probed the question of meaning
and its role in the organization of experience, the closer he came not
only to clarifying the significance of context but to explaining the
role of relevance.

The process by which meaning is constituted must be seen as a
form of behavior. As such, it is transactional in nature. As Dewey
put it, "Like all forms of behavior [it] is *transactional* in pattern in
that it is constituted by the cooperation or *working* together of
activities which, *when they are distinguished,* are referred respec-
tively to an organism in one respect and to environing conditions in
another regard."[44] (Dewey's italics.)

Theory-building runs the danger of separating something for
analysis that never again may be adequately reunited. A theorist can
become so engrossed in his analysis that he loses sight of the commonsense world where he began his work. Let us take an example.
W. I. Thomas articulated a valuable sociological insight when he
said, "If people define a situation as real, it is real in its consequences."[45] Subjective interpretations are social facts and have a
kind of power social scientists dare not ignore. But in pursuing this
insight, social scientists dare not forget the powerful and reciprocal
connection between subjective reality and the objective world. Subjective consciousness has its power, especially in the social sphere,
but it is not the only power alive in the world. There are forces over

which it has little control, forces of which subjectivity is itself a part. If we reify subjectivity and ignore the objective world in which subjectivity functions, we drastically distort reality. For example, a woman under certain conditions may believe herself pregnant. This erroneous belief may be so strong that it affects her biology. Menstruation may cease. She may feel periodically nauseous. Her breasts may become tender and may swell; in extreme cases, her abdomen may grow. She may feel the faint flutter of life in her womb. Her behavior may convince others of her pregnancy, and they will respond according to social custom. This and more can be accomplished by subjective beliefs that have real and powerful consequences. But subjective reality does not exhaust all reality nor does it necessarily overpower objective fact. The unfortunate lady of our example has changed significant aspects of her life through the power of belief. But she will not bear a child solely through the power of subjective thought.

Dewey tried to keep the power of objective reality clearly in mind (and in the minds of his audience) when he dealt with the question of meaning and relevance. He would have agreed with St. Augustine, who said that "truth dwells in the inner man." But Dewey would remind us that truth and reality are not exhausted there.

Some may argue that Schutz is less explicit than Dewey in this regard. However, I believe that Schutz did not ignore objective reality in his sociological theory or in his exploration of relevance. This study will make an effort to explain Schutz's position. By returning frequently to the question, it should clarify the role of objective fact in Schutz's theory of relevance.

Needless to say, the language Dewey uses in dealing with the question of relevance sometimes differs markedly from the highly technical language to which phenomenologists are prone. And it needs to be pointed out that Dewey never focused fully on the problems of relevance, scattering his insights instead through his voluminous work as topics to be examined on the way to other questions. Therefore, there is no easy access to his views on relevance, and we must roam the breadth of his writings to retrieve his ideas. But once this is done, we find a remarkable similarity between his views and those of Schutz.

This study will utilize the thoughts of both Dewey and Schutz on the problem of relevance. It will not simply juxtapose and compare the ideas of these two great thinkers, but will use their ideas to clarify the organization of human experience. Dewey and Schutz are uniquely suited to such a task, because they share a profound interest in experience. Yet they approach the topic via different philosophical perspectives and with decidedly different emphases. Thus, portions of both Dewey's and Schutz's works are overlooked frequently by their followers and critics and can be utilized profitably to clarify questions regarding the organization of experience. Their ideas can be brought together to allow the works of one to shed new light on the ideas of the other. For an example of such reciprocal clarification, Schutz's work on the problem of relevance is helpful in highlighting the significance of the pre-reflective elements of the field of consciousness. Armed with Schutz's clarification of this area, it becomes easier to find those portions of Dewey's work which address themselves to the pre-reflective. Similarly, it is possible to use the works of Dewey to clarify problematic portions of Schutz's theory, significantly the role of interest in experience. Using Dewey's thoughts in this way brings new clarity to Schutz's work on the problem of relevance.

The focus of this exploration will not attempt to do justice to the scope of the works and interests of Schutz and Dewey. But it will seek to discover the organizational processes alive in human experience, a topic of central importance to the philosophies of both men. Whatever differences may be found in the thoughts of these men— and there are many—it nevertheless can be claimed fairly that experience is the taproot from which their other ideas draw sustenance.

Guiding this work is the realization that Schutz, like Dewey, "constantly sought out what was common to the divergent currents of thought rather than what separated them."[46] Certainly a writer with another emphasis could show easily that Dewey and Schutz had important and numerous differences of opinions, differences which are significant to philosophy. Pragmatism is not just an American version of phenomenology, and no such claim is made here. But to overemphasize the differences is to distort the significant complementary areas which can serve as a basis for further dialogue between phenomenology and pragmatism. It is unfortunate that until recently such a dialogue has been woefully lacking.[47]

Having said we will not treat pragmatism and phenomenology as adversaries, it must be admitted that Schutz was not comfortable with pragmatism's naturalistic approach. He used the ideas of many pragmatists—notably, William James, George Mead, and John Dewey to a lesser extent—but he referred to their works more to make a specific point than to explore pragmatism in depth. Maurice Natanson's second doctoral dissertation, which Schutz directed, was a highly imaginative examination of George Herbert Mead. Natanson claims that Schutz drew from pragmatism as much as he did, "because he was trying in the 1940's to find an American expression for some of his ideas. By turning to James, Dewey, Whitehead, and George Santayana, Schutz was able to find an American way of introducing his students and reading audience to distinctively Husserlian problems."[48]

I believe this is much too narrow a perspective for a man of Schutz's wide intellectual interests and appreciations. While he was greatly indebted and dedicated to the thoughts of Husserl, he was never imprisoned by them. He was able to appreciate and use the thoughts of many other philosophers to widen and enrich his own perspectives. It is difficult to imagine that Schutz used American philosophy only as a vehicle to transport Husserlian ideas. Schutz was too open and thorough a scholar to employ such tactics.

This is not to imply that he was devoted to pragmatism. A few brief criticisms in his writing lend weight to Natanson's contention that "as a phenomenologist, Schutz could find relatively little [to agree with] in the kind of naturalism Dewey's position presupposes and involves."[49] Thus, many of the following claims that the ideas of Dewey and Schutz complement each other might not be granted by Schutz himself. We have to deal with his scattered criticisms of pragmatism to see if these arguments stand up fairly against them. Because such issues are often quite technical in nature, they will be confronted throughout this study as they become pertinent to the topic at hand.

3. The Philosophic Attitudes
of Dewey and Schutz

Man's paramount reality is not to be found in the realms of science, philosophy, or intellectualized religious study, but in the fundamental realm of everyday life, the everyday life-world. Schutz and Luckmann called it "that province of reality which the wide-awake and normal adult simply takes for granted in the attitude of common sense. By this taken-for-grantedness, we designate everything which we experience as unquestionable. . . ."[1] Within the *Lebenswelt*, the world is presented to us as self-evident and real. The structures of reality for man within the natural attitude, that attitude which characterizes his existence within the life-world, are prescientific and pretheoretical and serve as the fundament of theoretical and scientific thought.

To understand man in the everyday life-world is to explore the presuppositions which he takes for granted. To accomplish this, Schutz thought it necessary to examine the world at the point of its taken-for-grantedness by suspending what he called "the *epoché* of the natural attitude."[2] Within the natural attitude, man "does not suspend his beliefs in the existence of the outer world and its Objects. On the contrary," say Schutz and Luckmann, "he suspends every doubt concerning their existence."[3] Perhaps "suspends" is too intentional a word. Man in his everyday life seldom makes a conscious decision not to doubt his world: such wholesale doubt does not occur to him within the natural attitude. Nor does "reality" as a category occur to him, even when he is fully attentive. "*In the natural attitude,*" writes Edmund Husserl, "*there is at first (prior to reflection) no predicate 'real,' no genus 'reality.'*" (Husserl's italics.)[4] The objects of experience within the life-world are taken as real until the assumption of reality is in some manner contradicted. As William James stated, "Any object which remains uncontradicted is *ipso facto* believed and posited as absolute reality."[5] Within the natural attitude, objects are experienced as real until further notice.

Schutz called for detachment from the *epoché* of the natural attitude, for man to put beyond question some portions of his experience
of the world. As he stated in *Reflections*, "Since our purpose is the
description of the structure of Nature as taken for granted, it is exactly that kernel of our experience of Nature which we believe to be
self explanatory and not worth putting into question which we seek
to study." For example:

> When describing the structure of Nature as it appears to man
> living naïvely in his surroundings, we have to forget the teach-
> ings of Copernicus. . . . The natural system of reference for man,
> the unmoved and unmovable ground upon which . . . all possible
> movements are interpreted is the surface of the earth—the "pri-
> mal arch" . . . as Husserl called it. In man's naïve experience it
> does not *seem* that the sun "rises" in the east and "sets" in the
> west, it *is* so. [Schutz's italics.][6]

It has already been stated that Dewey recognized the need for
reflective detachment in philosophy. That argument can be expanded
somewhat, although he neither attempted nor accomplished the detailed structural mapping of the *Lebenswelt* which Schutz undertook.
Nevertheless, Dewey did anticipate many phenomenological concerns. As he pointed out in *Experience and Nature*, "The things of
primary experience are so arresting . . . that we tend to accept them
just as they are—the flat earth, the march of the sun from east to west
and its sinking under the earth."[7] Dewey was aware that the things
hidden beneath the *epoché* of the natural attitude have immeasurable
influence on what we experience and how we interpret our experience of the world. "The things which we take for granted without
inquiry or reflection are just the things which determine our conscious thinking and decide our conclusions." They are "certain [and]
assured. And this does not mean a mere feeling of certainty. It denotes not a sentiment, but a practical attitude. . . ."[8]

If man would understand the stock of knowledge on which his
actions are based, Dewey believed he must obtain a degree of detachment from "everything which is assumed without question,
which is taken for granted in our intercourse with one another and
nature. . . ." This is because man's "habitudes . . . lie below the level
of reflection" and are not easily brought into view.[9] "Actual experience," Dewey explained, "is such a jumble that a degree of distance
and detachment are a pre-requisite of vision in perspective. . . . A
withdrawal is necessary, unless [a thinker is] to be deafened by the

immediate clamor and blinded by the immediate glare of the scene."[10] It seems clear that Dewey wanted to detach himself from an attitude of certainty characterizing our everyday living.

An empirical investigation of the taken-for-granted nature of everyday experience is described by Dewey as a kind of "intellectual disrobing." As he puts it, "we cannot permanently divest ourselves of the intellectual habits we take on and wear when we assimilate the culture of our own time and place." But cultural progress and intellectual understanding demand "that we take some of them off, that we inspect them critically to see what they are made of and what wearing them does to us." From Dewey's perspective: "We cannot achieve recovery of primitive naïveté. But . . . a cultivated naïveté [is possible] through the discipline of severe thought." While Dewey acknowledged that it was "literally impossible to exclude that context of the non-cognitive but experienced subject-matter which gives what is *known* its import," he nevertheless contended that the noncognitive could be made the subject matter of our reflective gaze. "Attitudes themselves," he said, "may be made a special object of attention. . . ."[11] Thus, reflection is not simply reliving experience but a reconstruction and clear exploration of what is alive within experience. Merleau-Ponty makes this point by claiming that reflection "grasps its object as it comes into being and as it appears to the person experiencing it, with the atmosphere of meaning then surrounding it, and . . . tries to infiltrate into that atmosphere. . . ."[12] Dewey wished to penetrate that atmosphere with the sharp edge of reflective detachment. This detachment, made possible by acquiring a cultivated naïveté through reflection, is not exactly equivalent to the process of phenomenological bracketing as introduced by Husserl, but it avoids the pitfalls of Husserl's transcendental idealism.

Dewey rejected the notion that man could loosen his habitual ties with the world so completely he could transcend it. This agrees with Merleau-Ponty's insight that complete phenomenological reduction is not possible.[13] It is inconceivable that an individual could remove himself wholly from the world of his being and elevate himself to transcendent spectator. It is impossible for the entire context of our existence to be wrenched all at once from the background of consciousness. Portions of our lived world can be examined for insights into that context of meaningfulness which make judgments possible. But the entire *Lebenswelt*, that panoramic foundation of meaning, cannot be rendered visible all at once. Man cannot escape the "Platonic cave" and achieve transcendent insight into existence. He is not simply a being, but always a being in the world, and he must content himself with an understanding of meaningful existence rather than idealistic essences. It is to the credit of Dewey and of James that they have grasped this fact so foreign to Western philosophical tradition.[14] The life-world within the natural attitudes is fundamentally opaque and even in reflection will not give up its opacity totally. But careful reflection makes it possible to catch the constitutive powers of consciousness at work. We can view "the attitudes themselves" as they intend our world. But such insights come not all at once via transcendent idealism, but piece by piece through reflection.

It is imperative to understand that mere introspection is not identical with reflection. Reflection considers both man and world in an attempt to analyze their transactions. As Dewey noted long ago, introspection "assumes that something called 'consciousness' is an originally separate and directly given subject-matter and that it is also the organ of its own immediate disclosure of all its own secrets."[15] Consciousness is never so self-sufficient. It is found only as man and world interact. There is an "intrinsic connection of the self with the world," which is accomplished through the "reciprocity of undergoing and doing," said Dewey.[16] Man is never without a world. He cannot be specified independently of his world, anymore than his world is specifiable apart from his experience of it.

Schutz and Dewey share the belief that the taken-for-granted must be made thematic if we hope to understand human experience fully. Some might argue that pragmatism and phenomenology apply that "full understanding" to dramatically dissimilar ends, and that this constitutes a substantial difference between the two philosophies. They might contend that phenomenology's use of eidetic reduction leads ultimately to an idealistic transcendence of the everyday world. Pragmatism, by contrast, leads into the fold of mundane existence. The "egology" within Husserl's transcendent idealism assigned truth to the interior reaches of man. In the last paragraph of *Cartesian Meditations*, Husserl endowed the Delphic motto "know thyself" with new significance. "I must lose the world by epoché, in order to regain it by a universal self-examination," said Husserl. He went on to quote St. Augustine. "Do not wish to go out; go back into yourself. Truth dwells in the inner man."[17]

This metaphysics of the transcendent ego is a major concern of some phenomenologists, significantly Husserl, but not for Schutz. He was influenced deeply by Husserl, but he was not blindly loyal to all Husserl's ideas. It may have been Schutz's interests in the social sciences which led him out of Husserl's quagmire concept of the transcendental ego.

Schutz dropped his early attempts to achieve an egological perspective in the social sciences. He realized that man is in the world from the outset. Only by viewing him within the world of his existence can he be known at all. To do otherwise, said Dewey, is to set up a "hard and fast wall between the experiencing subject and that nature which is experienced. The self becomes not merely a pilgrim but an unnaturalized and unnaturalizable alien in the world."[18] Man is a participant in the world. He cannot be exiled to roam some unworldly realm. Schutz concluded in one of his last papers:

> We may say that the empirical social sciences will find their true foundation not in transcendental phenomenology, but in the constitutive phenomenology of the natural attitude. Husserl's signal contribution to the social sciences consists neither in his unsuccessful attempt to solve the problem of the constitution of transcendental intersubjectivity within the reduced egological sphere, nor in his unclarified notion of empathy as the foundation of understanding, nor, finally, in his interpretation of communities and societies as subjectivities of a higher order the nature of which can be described eidetically; but rather in the wealth of his analyses pertinent to the problems of the *Lebenswelt* and designed to be developed into a philosophical anthropology.[19]

It is fair to say that Schutz's sociology was not an effort to transcend human experience, unless one means that he was dedicated to achieving a deeper understanding of what experience entails. He would believe, as his student Peter Berger observed, that "sociology is justified by the belief that it is better to be conscious than unconscious and that consciousness is a condition of freedom."[20] This is a transcendence *into* human experience on a grander scale. This perspective makes it possible to be attentive to the operations of consciousness which work precognitively in everyday experience. It is possible to view not only what is known but the genesis of knowing itself. When we "trace the genesis of knowing," Dewey said, we are not only able to enrich "the subject matters of crude experience," but we are "prepared to understand what we are about on a grander scale, and to understand what happens even when we [are] the hapless puppets of uncontrollable fate."[21]

Therefore, Dewey and Schutz move us to an important understanding of philosophy's task. Reflection, no matter how radical, does not lead us to any final clarification of meaning or to the discovery of any ultimate foundation upon which all meanings finally rest. There will be no Platonic vision of ultimates for a philosopher who keeps man and world at the center of his understanding. To leave either or both of these behind while philosophizing is to abandon truth: truth must begin and end with man in the world. Truth and meaning are never ultimates but are always evolving in the process of man's being-in-the-world. The world (world-for-me) is then itself an evolving process. Philosophy progressively clarifies its meaning, explaining the process of human experience which makes meaning and truth possible. Experience of the world entails both reflective and pre-reflective, thematic and nonthematic elements. Philosophy must heed all these elements as experience unifies and organizes them.[22]

4. The Paramount Reality of the Everyday Life-World

THE IMMEDIATE sector of experience centers around the lived body.[1] Life is experienced in the here and now of *my* presence in the world. This is the zone of my working acts. All other zones, distant in time and space, will be coordinated with it in consciousness. The world is experienced with the lived body of the experiencer at its center. James pointed out that "the individualized self . . . is a part of the content of the world experienced." The individual is not an entity set apart but rather is engaged in the world. "The world experienced (otherwise called the 'field of consciousness')," James said, "comes at all times with our body at its centre, centre of vision, centre of action, centre of interest. The body is the storm centre. . . . Everything circles around it, and is felt from its point of view."[2]

The world of everyday life confronts man with an ordered reality. It is a world of facticity, a factual world of physical things, objectified ideas, and fellow men which offers resistance to us and on which we must act. "This world," Schutz tells us, "is to our natural attitude in the first place not an object of our thought but a field of domination. We have an eminently practical interest in it, caused by the necessity of complying with the basic requirements of our life."[3] The world of working is so named because it is the locus of my working acts. It is predominated by a practical attitude—Schutz called it the "pragmatic motive"—wherein I am concerned with interacting with the surrounding environment.

The world of working demands from us the greatest possible degree of attention (referred to in phenomenological terminology as the "highest tension of consciousness"). It is "an aleatory world" within which "existence involves, to put it baldly, a gamble. The world is a scene of risk," Dewey noted. "It is uncertain, unstable, uncannily unstable."[4]

The world of everyday life is the locus of man's paramount reality. It is a world where reality is most stable and, one might say carelessly, where reality is most real. But this needs some explanation. James informed philosophers long ago that each world of our experience is real in its own fashion while it is being attended to.[5] It is difficult to assign preeminence to any one reality, be it encountered in the world of art, dreams, religion, or hallucination. The centaur encountered in a daydream, the ghosts which invade the consciousness of Hamlet or Ebenezer Scrooge, are taken in consciousness as being neither more nor less real than, say, the horses or mortals encountered in everyday life. The difference is only to be found in the fashion we experience them. Objects taken as real in everyday life are subject to a verification that is absent in the other realms. The consequences of their reality are substantially different from those found in other finite provinces of meaning. The contextual arrangements in which they appear differ substantially also. Thus, it is possible to say that the world of work constitutes man's paramount reality, meaning only that the "things of sense," as James called them, "hold [a] prerogative position, and are the absolutely real world's nucleus."[6]

The foregoing does not suggest that perceptions of horses are the product of natural events while perceptions of centaurs are not. As Dewey explains, "The proposition that the perception of a horse is objectively valid and that of a centaur fanciful and mythical does not denote that one is a meaning of natural events and the other is not. It denotes," he says, "[only] that they are meanings referable to *different* natural events, and that confused and harmful consequences result from attributing them to the same events."[7] The next section will refer again to this topic in dealing with provinces of meaning other than that of everyday life.

The world of everyday life is intersubjective and given to us in childhood as meaningful. Its meanings derive largely from our predecessors and contemporaries and, relatively speaking, will live on with only slight alterations after we die. Thus, we assume that the world is seen by others much as we see it. From the viewpoint of the natural attitude, the world, says Schutz,

> is from the outset not the private world of the single individual but the intersubjective world, common to all of us, in which we have not a theoretical but an eminently practical interest. The world of everyday life is the scene and also the object of our actions and interactions. We have to dominate it and we have

to change it in order to realize the purposes which we pursue within it among our fellow men. We work and operate not only within but upon the world.[8]

In everyday life, man experiences his world as unified, and himself as unified in it. Language plays a significant part in this unification, as will be explained later. Suffice it now to quote Berger and Luckmann's observation that "language marks the co-ordinates of my life in society and fills that life with meaningful objects."[9] Implicitly and explicitly it constitutes the order and interpretation which society gives to experience.[10] Language originates in the realm of man's paramount reality. Its limitations are seen most readily when used to characterize other provinces of meaning. For example, language is often inadequate to replicate dreams, art, or love.

The everyday world is also characterized by a temporal structure which prearranges certain aspects of our daily existence and life-plans. We move in intersubjective time, universalized by clocks, calendars, work schedules, and a shared recognition of the sequential order of things. There are occasions when we leave the everyday life-world to enter another province of meaning where time structures are different. Re-entering the life-world requires effort. Where am I? What day is it? What am I doing here? These questions are often among the first posed by a person just regaining consciousness.

Dewey and Schutz share certain theoretical insights into the nature of experience. But they possess a useful difference of emphasis to which we can turn our attention now. Schutz observes that the reality confronted in everyday life is compelling. It does not require unending retesting; therefore, man generally can live with the assumption that what has worked in the past can be expected to work again and again in the future. For example, we know theoretically that all mechanical things are subject to failure. Nevertheless, we assume that our automobile will start in the morning, and we plan our departure for work with this taken for granted. We assume that clocks will continue to run forward, that until further notice gravity can be trusted to work today as it did yesterday.

We take something for granted only until further notice. This is why Dewey emphasizes the precarious nature of human existence. What man takes for granted is being contradicted constantly by events. His highest risks are in the world of working—a world, Dewey contends, of uncanny instability. Such contradictions punctuate life and propel man to conscious action, the intent of which is to rebuild a damaged portion of the taken-for-granted world. The structures of such reconstruction may not replicate the original: they may be very different from them or nearly identical. The point is that when notice is served, some portion of the taken-for-granted world becomes precarious. This notice serves as a prologue to action. Without contradictions, without instability, consciousness would not exist. The reverse is equally true. Consciousness would be impossible without taken-for-granted trivia.

When Schutz speaks of the stability of everyday reality and Dewey refers to its precarious nature, they may seem at variance at first. But each position implies and depends on the other. Life is a rhythm of harmony and discord, of unity, disunity, and unity reconstructed. This rhythm gives life to consciousness, for consciousness is the instrument of reconciliation between the expected and the unexpected.

Schutz's criticism of pragmatism will extend our understanding of the life-world. "The radical pragmatist," says Schutz in probable reference to Max Scheler but perhaps to Dewey as well, "tries to reduce any kind of knowledge to its usefulness for coming to terms with the surrounding world" or environment.[11] Dewey, of course, has been the target of such criticism for some time and the fault is partly his. Nevertheless, it is invalid to contend that Dewey based his theory of knowledge solely on man's quest to adapt to his surroundings. Such criticism would be directed more aptly at the social Darwinists. The criticism is understandable only because Dewey often uses examples which suggest this narrow focus. Think of his repeated references to men lost in the woods, to fingers burned and rivers forded. Criticism is also encouraged by the special meanings Dewey ascribes to such important words as "environment." It is to this latter topic we now turn. In digging out Dewey's meaning of "environment," we hope to show that Schutz's criticism is unwarranted if applied to Dewey. More important, it will extend our understanding of the life-world.

DEWEY AND THE TOTAL LIFE-WORLD

Dewey intended that the word "environment" mean a great deal more than the mere physical surroundings of an organism. He specifically states: "the words 'environment' [and] 'medium' denote something more than surroundings which encompass an individual. They denote the specific continuity of the surroundings with [man's] active tendencies." This suggests that environment exceeds that which is present both temporarily and physically. Dewey intends that "environment" stand for all that is necessary to life. This would include physical surroundings and extend through time and space to a great deal more. Environment includes all that affects man, all the things "that promote or hinder, stimulate or inhibit [his] living being" in the world.[12] He was talking about the totality of the world in which man lives. "We live and act," Dewey reminds us, "in connection with the existing environment, not in connection with isolated objects. . . ."[13] He suggests by this that "environment" should refer to something more than a world of things, to more than "the actual visible environment—the trees, rocks, etc., which man is actually looking at."[14] Nor does Dewey mean environment to be only that external to man. He contends, "the epidermis is only in the most superficial way an indication of where an organism ends and its environment begins. There are things inside the body that are foreign to it, and there are things outside of it that belong to it *de jure*, if not *de facto*. . . ."[15]

To be true to Dewey's definition, environment should not be limited to those portions of the world which man can see or touch or is conscious of. "The environment must be a larger environment than the visible facts; it must include things not within the direct ken of . . . man."[16] In language more like Schutz's, it must include not only that within man's actual reach but all within his "potential" or "attainable reach," his "restorable reach," even that situated in a "world beyond his reach" but which influences his existence.[17] Making that point, Dewey says that "the activities of [an] astronomer vary" not with that which is readily at hand, but "with the stars at which he gazes or about which he calculates." He summarizes his point concisely. The environment must include all that "*with which man varies.*" (Italics added.)[18]

When viewed in this light, we begin to see that it is misleading to talk about man's being *in* an environment if we mean only that man is surrounded by it. John Wild's discussion of the "human world" is more to the point. "I am in the world rather as in a field of care, as we speak of a woman as being in nursing, or a young man as in love."[19] Dewey puts it this way:

The statement that individuals live in a world means . . . that they live in a series of situations. And when it is said that men live *in* these situations, the meaning of the word "in" is different from its meaning when it is said that pennies are "in" a pocket or paint is "in" a can. It means . . . that interaction is going on. . . . The conception of *situation* and of *interaction* are inseparable from each other.[20]

Dewey contends that to understand man is to first understand that he interacts with everything constituting his world. Separation of man and world is to be found in almost all areas of human study. From Dewey's perspective, this has wreaked havoc on man's understanding of his own being. It is an inaccurate, or at least incomplete, vision of man's existence. Certainly we must concern ourselves with what in every sense is inside of man. But as Dewey said, "While this is necessary, it is not enough." We must extend our vision to include the ways in which man interacts "with what is called environment—if we are to obtain a genuine conception of the unity of the human being."[21] Thus, he does not introduce the concept of environment in order to have us separate it from man. For example, the antiquarian's job is to "establish . . . connections" with the remote epochs he is studying.[22] An antiquarian worthy of his profession must understand what constitutes the environment of his subjects, must see how his subjects interact with it, and must be attentive to the products of that interaction. In short, he must gear himself into their reality.

Keeping in mind what has been said about Dewey's conception of environment and interaction, we can see that Dewey was moving surprisingly close to the Husserlian concept of life-world, or "world of everyday life." The *Lebenswelt* has been defined as "the total sphere of experiences of an individual which is circumscribed by the objects, persons, and events encountered in the pursuit of the pragmatic objectives of living; the whole sphere of everyday experiences, orientations, and actions through which individuals pursue their interests and affairs. . . ."[23] If we take experience to mean the process of interaction between man and his world—as both pragmatism and phenomenology do—we can see that Dewey and Schutz share a concern for the *Lebenswelt* as an important object for philosophical study. Phenomenologists view the life-world as "the naively experienced, immediately perceived reality of everyday life as grasped and understood by men in the midst of their ordinary activities."[24] The life-world must be seen as extending beyond the paramount reality of the world of work. It encompasses this province of meaning but is not exhausted by it. It is the universe of man's experience and encompasses all of what James referred to as "sub-universes" and what Schutz preferred to call "finite provinces of meaning." The worlds of work, art, science, fantasy, and so on are bound together within the universe of the total life-world.

We have tried to show that the narrowness of focus Schutz attributed to pragmatism is unwarranted criticism if leveled at Dewey. It is erroneous to assert that Dewey limited his investigation of consciousness to the actions of man in the outer world struggling to meet his biological needs.[25] This kind of criticism results from taking Dewey's conception of environment entirely too narrowly. Ironically, Schutz encountered precisely the same criticism from people who narrowly perceived his term "world." Such people, said Schutz, are "obviously inclined to restrict this term [world] to the natural world which *surrounds* the self. . . . Yet it seems to us that to restrict the term merely to the surrounding world—that is, to Nature in the broadest sense (including not only the physical but also the social and cultural Universe)—would be a restriction hampering our further endeavors. World," Schutz insists, "is not only Nature (that is, the surrounding world), but any realm of intentional objects of our experience."[26] This seems close to the point Dewey was trying to make when he wrote, "the things with which a man *varies* are his genuine environment."[27] It is a fair conclusion that Dewey and Schutz shared not only an interest in the life-world, but that they shared a propensity to be misunderstood by those who mistakenly affix a narrow meaning to such key concepts as "environment" and "world."[28]

STRUCTURES OF THE TOTAL LIFE-WORLD

"The everyday life-world" is defined by Schutz and Luckmann as that "reality which the wide-awake and normal adult simply takes for granted in the attitude of common sense."[29] Within this domain, we confront what James referred to as the "paramount reality" of perceivable objects.[30] But the total "life-world embraces still more than the everyday reality," according to Schutz and Luckmann.

Man sinks into sleep, day after day. He relinquishes the everyday natural attitude in order to lapse into fictive worlds, into fantasies. He is able to transcend everydayness by means of symbols. Finally, as a special case, he may consciously modify the natural attitude. Now, we can conceive the concept of the life-world so broadly that it includes all modifications of attitudes and alertness—viz., the tension of consciousness present within the normal adult.[31]

For clarity's sake, we refer to the expanded version of the *Lebenswelt* as the total life-world. It encompasses not only the world of everyday life, but all the other sub-worlds of man's reality.

Within the everyday life-world are sub-universes (as James called them) or finite provinces of meaning (as Schutz preferred to label them). Each is characterized by "the unity of its own particular lived experience—viz., its cognitive style."[32] Hence, "we call a certain set of our experience a finite province of meaning if all of them show a specific cognitive style and are—*with respect to this style*—not only consistent in themselves but are also compatible with one another."[33]

In the concept of the cognitive style, Schutz includes the Bergsonian notion of "tensions of consciousness." The highest tension of consciousness is found in the condition of wide-awakeness which man adopts in the paramount reality of the world of work. From this terminus of a continuum, consciousness increasingly relaxes as man becomes less and less interested in gearing into and acting on the external world. "Sleep is complete *relaxation of consciousness* and is combined with complete *withdrawal from life.*" (Schutz and Luckmann's italics.)[34] Different provinces of meaning, then, incorporate different degrees of tension in consciousness.

The *dominant* form of spontaneity is another cognitive aspect of lived experience found in our multiple provinces of meaning. Schutz refers to it as the mode of conscious activity. "Daydreaming, for example, transpires in passivity, scientific work in acts of thought, everyday life in acts of performing."[35] The word "dominant" is important. Science naturally can entail elements of what Schutz calls "performing," but science is primarily, though in no sense exclusively, a thought process. Thus, it is dominated by theoretical explorations. This form of spontaneity is quite different from that found in daydreaming or in everyday life.

Provinces of meaning may be further characterized by special forms of *epoché*. Within the everyday life-world, we suspend all doubt about the existence of the outer world. Within philosophic or scientific thinking, we carefully bracket taken-for-granted portions of our world and open ourselves to other possibilities in detached observation. The accent of reality can be withdrawn from various layers of the world. This is accomplished within different provinces of meaning by utilizing their own special form of *epoché*.

A specific form of sociality belongs to each cognitive style. Within the world of dreams we are essentially alone. From this extreme point along a continuum, we move toward various forms of experiencing others. The most extensive experience of others occurs in face-to-face encounters in the everyday life-world, where "communication and intersubjectively related action are the rule."[36]

The form taken by the experience of self is also influenced by our cognitive style. Dreams may free us from biological or biographical restraints characterizing our existence within the paramount reality. Everyday life may confine our self-experience to some narrow aspect of total being—the role of bureaucrat, priest, or objective scientist. Within these narrow confines, we experience ourselves not in totality but in segments relevant to the task at hand. We see the world from the bureaucrat's point of view, restrict our vision to that domain, and catch glimpses of ourselves in its reflection. Religious or aesthetic forms of experience probably bring man closest to a total experience of himself. Each province of meaning, then, is characterized by a specific form of self-experience.

Finally, each cognitive style has its own time perspective. As was pointed out, the world of everyday life has a temporal perspective of objective time. "[This] outer time is measurable; there are pieces of equal length; there are minutes and hours" which can be segmented by mechanical instruments or the coercive rhythms of nature. Within another province—when a music lover, for example, listens attentively to Beethoven's Pianoforte Sonata in D Minor—the imposition of outer time means nothing. The listener, Schutz tells us "lives in a dimension of time incomparable with that which can be subdivided into homogeneous parts." Music unfolds step by step within a duration of inner time, Bergson's *durée*. This experience of inner time is "the very form of existence of music" which binds the listener together with composers and performers. "Although separated by hundreds of years," said Schutz, "[the beholder] participates with quasi simultaneity in [the composer's] stream of consciousness by performing with him step by step the ongoing articulation of his musical thought."[37] A theatrical performance offers still another time perspective. It is related to the temporal dimensions of the everyday world but unrestricted by the measurement of clocks or the revolution of the earth. Thus, a lifetime can be depicted in the span of a two-hour play. Each province of meaning, then, is endowed with its own temporal dimensions.

Schutz examines various finite provinces of meaning, elucidating the cognitive style peculiar to each. His work includes such orders of existence as dreams, fantasies, religious experience, art, scientific contemplation, play, and to a lesser extent, insanity.

By no means are these provinces the only to be found in life. Love, sexuality, drug experiences, mob mentality, and diversionary non-aesthetic experiences (television)—these are but a few which come readily to mind. As Schutz pointed out, "There are several [and] probably an infinite number of various orders of realities, each with its own special and separate style of existence."[38]

COMPATIBILITY AND INCOMPATIBILITY IN AND AMONG FINITE PROVINCES OF MEANING

Conceive finite provinces of meaning as holes in the fabric of the paramount reality of everyday life. Individuals slip into these holes, relaxing their grip on the everyday life-world. This need not always entail a total release from the social world. Many of these provinces are socially recognized and organized. Society offers official means for transcending the everyday world and entering another level or order of existence. For example, ushers guide us to our theater seats. The reality of the outside world fades as the lights dim and the play receives the accent of our attention and thus the accent of reality. At intermission, and again at the end of the play, we are ushered back into everyday life.

The movement between provinces of meaning—from daydreams to theoretical contemplation, for example—is experienced as a specific shock. Because of differences between the cognitive styles of separate provinces, the movement from one to another means letting go one perspective and assuming another. The transition is never totally smooth; seldom is it gradual. It is accomplished by a Kierkegaardian "leap" from one style of lived experience to another. To shift from one province to another, to replace the accent of reality, is to put objects in new relation to oneself and to one another. The mode of these differing contextual relationships is found in separate cognitive styles. We have indicated at some length that cognitive styles are characterized by differing tensions of consciousness, time perspectives, forms of experiencing the self, and forms of sociality. These styles are fundamentally incompatible with each other. This incompatibility explains the shock which accompanies our traffic between worlds.

The cognitive style characterizing a particular province of meaning is made possible by a compatibility of meaning within the province. "A finite province of meaning," say Schutz and Luckmann, "consists of meaning-compatible experiences." The loud noise which wrenches our attention from theoretical contemplation shifts our attention, because it is fundamentally incompatible with the other experiences of deep thought. "All experiences that belong to a finite province of meaning," they explain, "point to a particular style of lived experience—viz., a cognitive style. *In regard to this style*, they are all in mutual harmony and are compatible with one another."[39]

Schutz points out elsewhere that this compatibility of lived experiences exists only within a particular province.

> We have to emphasize that consistency and compatibility of experiences with respect to their particular cognitive style subsist merely within the borders of the particular province of meaning to which these experiences belong and upon which I have bestowed the accent of reality. By no means will that which is compatible within the province of meaning P be also compatible within the province of meaning Q. On the contrary, seen from P, which is supposed to be real, Q and all the experiences belonging to it would appear as merely fictitious, inconsistent, and incompatible, and *vice versa*.[40]

We can pull enough examples from our experiences to support Schutz's insight and render it understandable. Within the context of revolutionary fever, the world of humor may be rendered, unfortunately, not only irrelevant but meaningless. Monday night football may seem irrelevant nonsense from the viewpoint of a religious conversion experience. And the total *Lebenswelt* may be rendered absurd, as the existentialists never tire of informing us, from the perspective of oncoming death. If we grant these occasions, we do not totally accept Schutz's depiction of the multiple reality as described so far.

It is true that the context of an experience is immensely important to the cognitive style of that experience. But insisting that cognitive styles of separate provinces of meaning bear no relationship to, and are mutually exclusive of, each other can lead to some misunderstanding of the process of experience. It also fails to explain aesthetic religious experiences which draw meaning from multiple realms.

The question which confronts us now is, Just how different are the experiences within the separate provinces of meaning? If we allow ourselves to believe that man is confronted with multiple realities, bearing no relationship to each other and mutually incompatible, we end up with a peculiarly bifurcated world. Yet the total life-world of man is perceived as more harmonious than discordant. Although we traverse the boundaries of our multiple reality structures each day of our lives, it generally is acknowledged that our experiences within these various structures are not totally unrelated. The stuff of our daydreams may be distortions of everyday life, but they are not totally unrelated to it. The daily world is the paramount reality, serving as the home base for all other provinces of meaning. "In relation to other provinces of reality with finite meaning structure," say Schutz and Luckmann, "the everyday life-world is the primary reality."[41] It serves as home base for all other reality structures. It stands as the "archetype of our experience of reality. All the other provinces of meaning may be considered as its modifications."[42]

We can grasp the significance of this statement by taking advantage of Dewey's somewhat different approach to this topic. Once again we have to contend with the criticism Schutz leveled against pragmatism. This is necessary in order to show the essential if limited connection between various provinces of meaning.

"Pragmatism," said Schutz, "is not a philosophy dealing with the totality of human existence, but a *description* of our living on the *level of the unquestioned paramount reality*." (Italics added.)[43] Had Schutz dedicated an essay specifically to Dewey, we could tell if he wished to include him in this criticism. Richard Zaner, who painstakingly edited the book from which this criticism was drawn, believes that "much of the work of James, especially the early James, would not fall under that criticism, nor much of Dewey."[44] Lacking clear information exempting Dewey, we have to deal with the criticism as if it were directed at him.

Dewey indeed placed great, although not exclusive, emphasis on the importance of man's mental conduct and working acts.[45] Through these acts, man experiences the outer world and intentionally affects his surroundings. The world of working by no means exhausts the possibilities of man's existence, but it does constitute his paramount reality. It generates its own cognitive style and surrounds and permeates all other finite provinces of meaning. From this realm, man gears himself into the outer world and communes with his fellow man. In this world, social facts are experienced as having coercive power, a power which man ignores at his peril.[46]

It would be wrong to contend that Dewey's interest in the structure of man's paramount reality ended at mere description. As early as the turn of the century, he was calling for, even embarking on, a philosophical inquiry into "the structural arrangements of mind." He criticized the social sciences for the dual error of judging "the savage mind" by criteria supplied by the habits of modern man and ignoring all that which is taken for granted by those living in primitive society. He bemoaned the tendency of the social scientists to accumulate "static facts" which were "torn loose from their context in social and natural environment and heaped miscellaneously together" to be measured against "a fixed scale" supplied by the "present civilized mind" which "is taken as a standard."[47]

Nor is it correct to say that Dewey was only interested in what constituted the paramount reality of the savage mind. His 1902 article on this subject not only examined what constituted primitive man's world of paramount reality but dealt with the ways the concerns of the province were "carried over into various activities" dominated by other finite provinces of meaning. Having established, for example, that hunting was the dominant interest of one group of Australian aborigines, he proceeded to show how that "central interest" could establish itself as the "ground pattern" for such other provinces of meaning as play, language, drama, courtship, art, etc.[48]

Schutz contended that our paramount reality serves as a "home base for all other levels of reality," which are interpreted as deviations from it.[49] It is the archetype of all other sub-universes.[50] Dewey would agree, but he would want to show the degree to which home-base reality influences other provinces of meaning. Dewey's emphasis on the ways paramount reality interconnects with other provinces of meaning should be significant for phenomenologists. As Schutz has said, "Language, myth, religion, art, etc. . . . are essential elements of the *Lebenswelt* and accordingly of highest interest to the social sciences." In his own way, Dewey was attempting a theory which would meet Schutz's criteria for dealing with "the problem of multiple levels of reality and their interconnection, and with the foundation of all of them upon the paramount reality of the *Lebens-welt*."[51]

Dewey also alluded to another interest—the degree to which the paramount reality of primitive men extends not only through various provinces of meaning but through time and history as well. He described how the ground-pattern reality of the hunter's world could be handed down and "deeply embedded in [the] consciousness" of later generations.[52] He felt sure there were traits of modern man which were neither clearly relevant to, nor connected with, his present existence, but which could be traced to origins in past generations.

The essay as a whole called for careful study of the "scheme or pattern of the structural organization of mental traits" which he claimed would supply "an important method for the interpretation of social institutions and cultural resources" and would constitute "a psychological method for sociology."[53] This seems to amount to a metasociological concern so typical of Schutz's work, namely, "the delineation of the subject matter of sociology."[54]

Why is it that Dewey is accused of having a narrow focus, of not attending to the totality of man's existence? The answer is found in Dewey's concern with the importance of "paramount reality" and the ways this reality affects man's experience of other realms. This, I have tried to show, does not mean that Dewey was interested in the realm of paramount reality to the exclusion of all other finite provinces of meaning. It does mean that Dewey was fearful of over-emphasizing the distinctive character of man's experience within these provinces to the degree any clear picture of the unity of human existence would be lost. Acknowledging the differences between immediate, mundane, scientific, religious, and aesthetic experience, Dewey was quick to prove that although these differences were large, they were more of degree and emphasis than of kind. Dewey wrote, "The difference between the esthetic and the intellectual is . . . one of the place where emphasis falls in the constant rhythm that marks the interaction of the live creature with his surroundings." *Art as Experience* deals quite thoroughly with the nature of the aesthetic experience, but Dewey was unwilling to sever the aesthetic from other modes of experience by insisting upon unduly strict lines of demarcation. "Esthetic emotion," he wrote, "is . . . something distinctive and yet not cut off by a chasm from other and natural

emotional experiences, as some theorists . . . have made it to be."[55]
For Dewey and Schutz, the everyday life-world is the founding level
of all meaning.

Dewey emphasized the need for philosophy to "return to the
things of crude or macroscopic experience . . . of common every-day
life."[56] This emphasis is reminiscent of Husserl's insistence that philosophy move back to the things themselves. Dewey believed that
through a "return to experienced things, . . . the meaning, the significant content, of what is experienced gains an enriched and expanded force. . . ."[57] Such an emphasis keeps philosophy from being
isolated from real life, a concern Dewey shared with the philosophers of phenomenology.[58] It also guards man against the mischie-
vous notion that "mental attitudes, *ways* of experiencing, [are to be]
treated as self sufficient and complete in themselves, as that which
is primarily *given*, the sole original and therefore indubitable data."
(Dewey's italics.)[59] He emphasized further that all forms of human
experience have generic similarities, a fact easily lost if, for example,
the experience of "art is remitted to a separate realm, where it is cut
off from that association with the materials and aims of every other
form of human effort. . . ." Thus, the task of any philosophical inquiry
into art does not stop at showing the distinctive characteristics of
aesthetic experience. Its task must be "to restore continuity between
the refined and intensified forms of experience that are works of art
and everyday events. . . ."[60] Dewey's statement on art is applicable
equally to other modes of man's experience. For example, Dewey
speaks of dreams:

> We dream, but the material of our dream life is the stuff of our
> waking life. Revery is not . . . wholly detached from the ob-
> jects of purposeful action and belief. . . . Its objects consist of
> the objects of daily concern subjected to a strange perspective,
> perverted in behalf of a bias. Such empirical facts as these
> [are] fatal to any theory which seriously asserts the wholesale
> irrelevance of the material of consciousness to the things of the
> actual world. Irrelevance exists, but it is relative and specifi-
> able.[61]

Dewey's point is that the world of everyday life is the "paramount
reality" of man, the final court of appeals. Other provinces operate
with differing cognitive styles and present us with realities of substantially different orders, but the sensory world must always remain

with us on the fringe. No matter how real we regard the perceptions of other provinces, a still greater reality is always peripherally present. No matter how lost we become in a play or in our private fantasies, we never totally lose awareness of our lived body and its surrounding physical environment. The reverse does not hold true. Fictive worlds may remain on the horizons of consciousness for a time but in most cases will fade eventually, as if "bullied out of existence" by a stronger, more stable reality.[62]

Perceptions of our various provinces of meaning are abstracted from the paramount reality of everyday life. Ultimately, we must return to this reality, often bringing back the products of our mental excursions. Scientific or philosophical, the products of theoretical contemplation must be returned to the primary world for verification. This was a constant concern for Dewey, one he well might have drawn from James. "A conception," said James, "[if it is] to prevail, must *terminate* in the world of orderly sensible experience." It cannot merely drift as a "disconnected rarity" if it is to remain the object of our regard. (James's italics.)[63] It must be granted worldly facticity, if it is not to float away out of sight and out of mind. Schutz's work confirms these points. Dewey's thoughts have been used here only to clarify further how paramount reality affects other provinces of meaning.

Schutz's original point was that the various provinces of meaning are intrinsically incompatible. With Dewey's thoughts in mind, this becomes clearer. The hobgoblins of our dream world are a useful example of this disunity. They appear to us as distorted worldly shapes, endowed in varying degrees with distortions of worldly intents. They stand as grotesque abstractions of objects found in everyday life. Awakening in fright, we find their reality—fixed firmly in dream a moment ago—gravely challenged. The shadows on our bedroom wall momentarily may confirm their existence as we grope for the light in the half-sleep which straddles both worlds. With illumination, all semblance of their reality fades. They are unbelievable and perhaps in a very short time will fade from memory. The everyday life-world offers no hooks for their existence. They fail to fit in with any system of meanings offered by the world of paramount reality. Thus, the dream world draws on the everyday life-world, but it is experienced on its own terms and with its own cognitive style. The hobgoblins of our dreams are incompatible with the hobgoblins of everyday life.

The reality of everyday life is paramount. That which cannot find compatibility within this realm must fade altogether from existence or remain confined to its own finite province. Hobgoblins may recur night after night in dreams. Sleep confirms their reality, awakening to full consciousness disconfirms it. But the hobgoblins constituted a *real dream, a genuine reality*. As we awaken, our experience may be translated from one province to another, although this is never accomplished without some distortion. The primitive society which views dreams as windows on the future, or the modern society (since Freud) which views them as windows to the vortex of past and present, may translate the substance of dreams into messages which can exist comfortably within the meaning structures of the everyday life-world. But hobgoblins as messages, as signs of a foreboding future or an unhappy past, do not possess the same meaning which they carried in a dream world where hobgoblins were experienced as hobgoblins. Translated into everyday life, they may be just as frightening as in the dream, but they are frightening in a different way. They have achieved a new relationship to the observer and thus have a wholly new meaning for him.

To illustrate the same point, centaurs exist in our everyday world, but in a relationship different from our dreams. In dreams they are believed to be real. They exist as centaurs. In everyday life, they are a category to which this reality does not apply. They cohere within a system of such other fictive phenomena as Pegasus and satyrs.[64] Again we find certain objects being shared by various provinces of meaning, each province utilizing and organizing the object according to different cognitive styles. Thus, the centaur of our dream changes meaning when we move into the context of the everyday life-world. It bears a different relationship to us. Although the everyday life-world is the ultimate source from which all provinces borrow objects and meaning, we have to conclude that the provinces remain basically incompatible.

We have discussed the fundamental differences between cognitive styles, the internal harmony within each finite province of meaning, the disharmony between provinces and the home-base nature of paramount reality. It is now possible to make one other point. Not only do we move many times daily between competing provinces of meaning, Schutz contends we can also live simultaneously within multiple provinces.[65]

Schutz illustrates this point. He suggests that while he is writing his essay on relevance, he is preoccupied with theoretical contemplation. This realm is his primary focal activity, the theme of his conscious awareness. But other activities, involving other portions of his attention, are carried on simultaneously. Assume he is writing at an outdoor picnic table near his Colorado vacation retreat. One hand grasps a ballpoint pen and transcribes thoughts on a yellow pad of legal-size paper. The other hand holds the pad and guards it against the light breeze blowing across the mountain where he sits. These activities go on habitually. They do not become a thematic concern unless interrupted by some trouble—the pen runs out of ink, a pain develops in his hand, a sudden gust of wind tears at his writing tablet. As he writes, he tries to clarify his thoughts on relevance. He searches for words, builds sentences, and orders them into paragraphs. All of this is done sub-thematically, until a problem demanding greater attention arises.

These varying activities—theoretical contemplation, language use, the physical act of writing—occur in seeming unity. However, Schutz emphasizes their quasi-independence from each other as activities. He acknowledges their clear interrelationship. What is written depends upon what language is presented: this is determined in turn by what occurs in theoretical contemplation. Theoretical contemplation on the problem of relevance is the primary focus on which other activities depend for the time being. But each activity differs in mode of operation. Schutz is "living" in the realm of theoretical contemplation, and his mental activity is dominated by the cognitive style belonging to that realm. However, he is engaged simultaneously in the habitualized, automatic activities of writing and translating thoughts into appropriate language. These activities operate with different cognitive styles and depend on different systems of relevance. Different levels of our personality are involved. To use Dorion Cairn's terminology, man is "busied" with each activity in quite dissimilar ways.

The thematized problem of relevance is Schutz's central interest. But the habitual activities of writing and language use are on its horizon. He explains the paradox of their relationship and independence by comparing it to the "counterpointal structures" found in music. "What I have in mind," said Schutz, "is the relationship between two independent themes simultaneously going on in the same flux or flow of music; or, more briefly, the relationship of counterpoint. The listener's mind may pursue one or the other, take one as the main theme and the other as the subordinate one, or vice versa. . . ."[66]

Thus, it is possible for the habitual, quasi-automatic activities of writing, walking, driving a car, etc., to be relegated to the horizons of consciousness while attention is paid primarily to the thematic concern of theoretical contemplation. The secondary actions are but sub-systems of the primary activity, internally systematized and characterized by their own cognitive style. Dewey referred to them as habits. Early in *Human Nature and Conduct* he said:

> The word habit may seem twisted somewhat from its customary use when employed as we have been using it. But we need a word to express that kind of human activity which is influenced by prior activity and in that sense acquired; which contains within itself a certain *ordering or systematization* of minor elements of action; which is projective, dynamic in quality, ready for overt manifestation; and which is *operative in some subdued subordinate form* even when not obviously dominating activity. [Italics added.][67]

CONCLUDING REMARKS

The length of this chapter makes it appropriate to review the major contentions and indicate their importance for what follows. The first section introduced the everyday life-world as man's paramount reality—the world in which physical things reside, where my lived body has its being. I feel my physical presence and locomotive power in this world, and I make a physical difference in my environment here. In this world, I find resistance to my efforts which must be overcome. From here I gear myself into the outer world—a world shared with others like myself and with products of my actions and theirs. Until further notice, this world accepts reality as self-evident and real. It is also the scene of continual risk, and as Zaner has put it, "at once the framework and the object of my actions."[68]

The second section extended the life-world beyond that confronted in the working world of everyday life. With Dewey's conception of environment as a point of departure, it contended that the total life-world includes not only our working world, but all those things with which man varies. It includes all the situations man finds himself in during his lifetime. And most important, it includes not only those factors within man often called "subjective," but also the social facts and physical things of the objective world outside.

Examining the characteristics of various structures of the total life-world, the third section showed that different provinces of meaning are characterized by differing cognitive styles. The everyday world has a cognitive style of its own and can be referred to as a finite province of meaning. Within this fabric of meaning are woven other finite provinces, each with its own cognitive style. When all provinces of meaning are considered together, including the province of paramount reality (the everyday life-world), they form the total life-world.

The fourth section illustrated the relationships existing within and among these various provinces. Their degree of incompatibility was discussed in relationship to the "shock" an individual experiences as he moves from one province to another. Dewey's insights into the interrelationship of experience allowed us to modify the notion of incompatibility. Such modification made it possible to explore simultaneous existence within multiple provinces of meaning.

Having pointed to where we have been, we must now point briefly in the direction we will be going. The question of multiple realities came to Schutz by way of James's *Principles of Psychology*.[69] Schutz wished to free James's insights from their psychological setting and to examine them in the fuller context of human experience. He tried to clarify and delineate further the sub-worlds to which James had referred and Husserl had incorporated under the headings of "unities of sense" and "meaning." He also attempted to clarify James's notion of paramount reality. Beyond this task, however, lay other important questions. How are these unities of meaning organized and constituted? What principles can be uncovered to account for placing the accent of reality within the context of one province rather than within another? And once placed, what is the organization of human experience as it unfolds within the framework of the province of meaning held paramount? In answering these questions we are confronted, as was Schutz, with the problem of relevance.[70]

We are not engaged simultaneously in every portion of the world of work. Nor are we concerned even peripherally with more than a small fraction of our finite province of meaning at one time. Our interests make us attentive to only small sectors of the world at any given moment. Man is a selective being, and the agency of selection seems to be man's interest. We daydream only as daydreaming holds our interest; when interest wanes, our attention passes to other things. Interests are related to the projects we have at hand. Because we are interested in a general project, certain things relevant to the project become interesting to us. If the boat is leaking and I am interested in survival, I become interested in how to make the pumping equipment operate more efficiently.

The next chapter will detail more sufficiently this line of analysis. Suffice it now to point out that the analysis just presented entails, among other things, a bothersome circularity: interest accounts for our attention to the project at hand and is also derived from it. But where do projects come from? To say they are formed always in total subjectivity is dangerous solipsism. To contend they are simply there, beckoning to man, strangely alienates man from interaction with the world. As Zaner has pointed out: "Each of my projects at hand is itself determined by something—and it is to this something that Schutz addresses himself with his conception of 'relevances.' The concept of 'interest' . . . is not only too ambiguous to articulate the principle involved here, it is also not entirely accurate inasmuch as it is too psychologistic. What is at stake, indeed, is a *principle of structuralization of the lifeworld itself*, a principle that is also determinative for my various interests and plans within the lifeworld in the sense that it is what accounts for 'why' I turn to 'this' rather than to 'that' at 'this' time in my life, in the course of 'this' action." (Zaner's italics.)[71]

The question of relevance will be examined shortly. But we will have to deal first with three other subjects intricately linked to that notion—the field of consciousness, typification and background, and subject-object unification in situation.

5. The Foundations of Experience

By THE VERY NATURE of attention, man cannot be attentive at any moment to all that is available to his consciousness. It is a terrifying fantasy indeed to imagine a mind totally receptive to everything in memory and world.[1] "It is impossible," Dewey said, "to imagine a living creature coping with the entire universe all at once."[2] Man is able to deal with the world because he is able to discriminate, to sort and typify his perceptions, to give meaning to his experience, to retain the *epoché* of the natural attitude in regard to past experiences, and to separate that which seems relevant to the immediate problem from that which is not. Schutz directed a great deal of effort toward clarifying these processes which allow the mind to be attentive to its world. His *Reflections on the Problem of Relevance* deals with these processes of consciousness and proceeds to what are perhaps the more basic questions: What determines our projects at hand? Which motivational relevance structures guide our activities? How is experience organized?

The term "relevance structures" refers to the subjective mind as it is organized in, and affected by, a situation. It includes what the mind brings to a situation and prefigures the way consciousness greets, interprets, acts on, and is influenced by, the world. The concept of relevance rests on other, interrelated concepts—field of consciousness, typification and background, subject-object unification in situation. We must deal with these, at least superficially, before we can delve directly into relevance and its attendant problems.

THE FIELD OF CONSCIOUSNESS

Through typification, language, and memory, man is able to retain and order much of his past experience. A great deal is lost of course, and that which is retained changes continually.[3] But certain experiences remain and fund what Schutz called our "stock of knowledge" and what Dewey (following James) referred to as our "stock of meanings."[4] Not everything ordered and retained in our stock of knowledge is presented to us at any given time. Only that deemed relevant to "this" situation is immediately at hand. Thus, in any moment of inner time our field of consciousness is made up of a thematic kernel—a problem on which our ray of attention has been cast—in the center of a surrounding horizon. Our existing knowledge and perceptions of the environment constitute the horizon, and these are ordered by gradations of relevance in relation to what is thematic. "If we consider the entire field," said Dewey,

> from bright focus through the fore-conscious, the "fringe," to what is dim, sub-conscious, "feeling," the focus corresponds to the point of immediate need, of urgency; the "fringe" corresponds to things that just have been reacted to or that will soon require to be looked after, while the remote outlying field corresponds to what does not have to be modified, and which may be dependably counted upon in dealing with immediate need.[5]

A great deal is to be included in what James called the "fringes" of our field of consciousness, as they radiate with increasing dimness from what is clear and close to the kernel of concern. Schutz speaks of looking at the cherry tree in his garden: "The tree refers to my garden, the garden to the street, to the city, to the country in which I am living, and finally to the whole universe. Every perception of a 'detail' refers to the 'thing' to which it pertains, the 'thing' to other things over [and] against which it stands out and which I call a background."[6]

The physical nature of this example should not mislead us—Schutz was not speaking merely of physical "things." Dewey uses another example to make this point:

> The scope and content of the focused apparency have immediate dynamic connections with portions of experience not at the time obvious. The word which I have just written is momentarily focal; around it there shade off into vagueness my typewriter, the desk, the room, the building, the campus, the town, and so on. *In* the experience, and in it in such a way as to *qualify* even what is shiningly apparent, are all the physical features of the environment extending out into space no one can say how far, and all the habits and interests extending backward and forward in time, of the organism which uses the typewriter and which notes the written form of the word only as temporary focus in a vast and changing scene. [Dewey's italics.][7]

Dewey refers here not only to the "physical features of the environment" but to the more clearly "subjective" elements of habit and interest. These elements arrange themselves on the horizons of consciousness according to gradations of clarity and dimness. What Dewey calls systems of "habits and interests" Schutz refers to as "relevance structures."[8] As Schutz said, they form the background against which the object of our attention stands out. Dewey makes the same point, but warns that what is on the horizon is not passive in consciousness but has a "dynamic connection" with the kernel or what he calls "focused apparency." As Dewey said, the things which form the horizon are

> the capital with which the self notes, cares for, attends, and purposes. In this substantial sense, mind forms the background upon which every new contact with surroundings is projected; yet "background" is too passive a word, unless we remember that it is active and that, in the projection of the new upon it, there is assimilation and reconstruction of both background and what is taken in and digested.[9]

Dewey clarifies his often-repeated contention that the objects of our attention do not appear in a vacuum, but rather within a field:[10]

> In actual experience, there is never any such isolated singular object or event; *an* object or event is always a special part, phase, or aspect, of an environing experienced world—a situation. The singular object stands out conspicuously because of its especially focal and crucial position at a given time in determination of some problem of use or enjoyment which the *total* complex environment presents. There is always a *field* in which observation of *this* or *that* object or event occurs. [Dewey's italics.][11]

Both Dewey and Schutz insisted that the kernel and the horizon are not to be thought of dualistically. These two elements of experience are interrelated, each owing its existence to the presence of the other. They are mutually affecting within a field of consciousness. To account adequately for human experience, it is necessary to take both these aspects into account and recognize their connection. Schutz makes these same points.

> Phenomenological analysis shows that . . . we do not have original experiences of isolated things and qualities, but that there is rather a field of our experiences within which certain elements are selected by our mental activities as standing out against the

background of their spatial and temporal surroundings; that within the through and through connectedness of our stream of consciousness all these selected elements keep their halos, their fringes, their horizons.[12]

Schutz believed that understanding the "mechanisms of pre-predicative judgment" will be achieved only by investigating the "mental processes in which and by which pre-predicative experience has been constituted."[13] "Relevance structures" and "horizons" are concepts central to this investigation.

Dewey, too, recognized the need for such study of "the vague and extensive background [which] is present in every conscious experience." As we have already pointed out, he warns that such study is complicated by "the dim and total background consciousness of every distinct thought" that is so "taken for granted" it is indistinguishable to us in everyday activities. Nevertheless, he contended that the "one great mistake in the orthodox psychological tradition is its exclusive preoccupation with sharp focalization to the neglect of the vague shading off from the foci into a field of increasing dimness."[14] He believed the disciplines of philosophy and the social sciences should undertake such a study.

The concept of horizon carries paradoxical implications. Helmut Kuhn has noted that the horizons are always present in consciousness, "limiting the totality of given things," framing them into contextual wholes.[15] Schutz stated that "no object is perceived as an insulated object; it is from the outset perceived as 'an object within its horizon' . . . of typical familiarity and preacquaintanceship."[16] He was contending that what is new must exist within the context of what is already known. By itself, this suggests that horizons can function to inhibit innovation. As Dewey frequently lamented, this is indeed a possibility. The habits which form our horizons can "possess us, rather than we them."[17] Man can become rutted in the grooves of his habits.[18] Through acts which Sartre would label "bad-faith," man may choose to live within fixed horizons.[19] As Dewey wrote, "Men still want the crutch of dogma, of beliefs fixed by authority, to relieve them of the trouble of thinking and the responsibility of directing their activities by thought."[20] It is clear that while horizons are necessary to consciousness, they may also inhibit the inherent potentials of consciousness.

However, it is important to emphasize that horizons are only potential, not inherent, inhibitors of consciousness. To quote Kuhn again, "By its very nature every horizon is 'open'. . . . We are constantly invited to transcend the boundaries of our field of vision."[21] Within limits, man can choose to explore his horizons. He can make the taken-for-granted portions of horizons thematic, reorganizing his stock of knowledge at hand and discarding habits no longer warranted. Thus, habits and horizons are both limiting and liberating. As Dewey said:

> By a seeming paradox, increased power of forming habits means increased susceptibility, sensitiveness, responsiveness. Thus even if we think of habits as so many grooves, the power to acquire many and varied grooves denotes high sensitivity, explosiveness. Thereby an old habit, a fixed groove if one wishes to exaggerate, gets in the way of the process of forming a new habit while the tendency to form a new one cuts across the same old habit. Hence, instability, novelty, emergence of unexpected and unpredictable combinations. The more an organism learns—the more, that is, the former terms of a historic process are retained and integrated in this present phase—the more it has to learn, in order to keep itself going. . . .[22]

Dewey and Schutz believe it is the pre-predicative or pre-reflective collision of habits which constitute problems and trigger consciousness.[23]

A more complete investigation of the structuring of the field of consciousness is beyond the scope of this study. Our purposes were to introduce the rudiments of the concept so it can be referred to later and to indicate that Dewey and Schutz agreed closely, insofar as the concept was developed here. Differences exist, but they lie outside present purposes and are not central to the argument.

TYPIFICATION AND BACKGROUND

Everything in the horizons of consciousness is ordered by a process which Schutz, following Husserl, calls typification. An infant is born with a total naiveté and perceives the surrounding world "as one great blooming, buzzing confusion."[24] His world exists totally in the foreground, without benefit of a background of previous experiences. In lower animals, instincts act as a sort of background; by biologically assigning significance to various parts of the world, they help to order what otherwise would be chaotic. Such theorists as Helmuth

Plessner and Arnold Gehlen have pointed out that man is born relatively free of these instinctive imperatives and through consciousness must order the world.[25] (Piaget has called it moving from chaos to cosmos.)[26] The theory of typification gives insight into how this process works. Classifying the things of the environment by types achieves a degree of order. Experiences can be labeled and kept in mind. Referring new experiences to previous ones permits typing and interpretation. Through what Husserl called "synthesis of identification," the new can be ordered by the old. Or as Schutz put it, "Actual experiences are matched with or superimposed upon the types of the already experienced material."[27] Typification systems form what some have called man's second nature. It is what Dewey, following Walter Lippman, has termed "a secondary pseudo-environment, which affects every item of traffic [in] dealing with the primary environment."[28]

Dewey came to conclusions very similar to the phenomenological conception of typification. He wrote about "standards of reference" and "standardized meanings" which "enable us to generalize, to extend and carry over our understanding from one thing to another." Conceptions, he claimed, "economize . . . intellectual effort," because "they represent [a] whole class or set of things." We need not hold every independent item in mind as a separate entity. "Conceptions *standardize* our knowledge. They introduce solidity into what would otherwise be formless, and *permanence* into what would otherwise be shifting." (Dewey's italics.)[29] Dewey wrote elsewhere: "To classify is, indeed, as useful as it is natural. The indefinite multitude of particular and changing events is met by the mind with acts of defining, inventorying and listing, reducing to common heads and tying up in bunches."[30]

In referring to James's example of the buzzing confusion of an infant's world, Dewey pointed out that all truly unique (not readily typifiable) experiences are perceived by man, regardless of age, as "blurred and confused." The reason is that "the usual marks that label things so as to separate them from one another are lacking" in situations which are "really new and strange." Foreign languages are an example, said Dewey. We encounter them for the first time as mere "jabberings and babblings in which it is impossible to fix a definite, clear-cut, individualized group of sounds." Factory work for example, seems to be "a meaningless medley" to the uninitiated.

And "All strangers of another race proverbially look alike to a visiting foreigner." Summing up, Dewey wrote, "The problem of the acquisition of meanings by things . . . is thus the problem of introducing (a) *definiteness*, or *distinction*, and (b) *consistency, coherence, constancy* or *stability* of meaning into what is otherwise vague and wavering." (Dewey's italics.)[31] If man is able to see how things are different, he must first grasp how things are the same. Dewey's examples of typification illustrate that this is no contradiction. By breaking things into types of samenesses, we are able to distinguish the separate entities of the buzzing confusion of the unknown.

Although it needs no elaboration here, it should be pointed out that more than physical things of the world become typified in consciousness. Behavior patterns such as roles and everyday routines, spatial relationships, temporality, belief systems, institutions—all things which constitute man's reality (or to remake Dewey's point, all things with which man varies)—exist in consciousness as typified.[32] Were this not so, consciousness itself would not exist. To quote Dewey again: "We bring to the simplest observation a complex apparatus of habits, of accepted meanings. . . . Otherwise observation is the blankest of stares, and the natural object is a tale told by an idiot, full only of sound and fury."[33] Typicality is not simply a result of experience. It is the heart of its very structure and gives life to its epistemological possibilities. It is prior and essential to experience.

The conceptions of horizon and typification combine to bring clarity to the notion of "background" alluded to earlier. Both Schutz and Dewey understood that the thematic portions of consciousness exist by virtue of relationship to that which is on the horizon. In words common to pragmatism, some portion of a situation must remain unproblematic (horizontal), when a problem arises within it. Dewey said, "There is always something unquestioned in any problematic situation. . . ."[34] Charles Morris made the same point when he wrote, "Not everything can be problematic at once; problems can be solved only within a context in which some objects and meanings and beliefs are accepted without question."[35] Of course, Dewey recognized that what is unproblematic in one situation may be thematic in another.[36] He clearly agrees with Schutz that something is taken for granted only until further notice, or as he might have put it, until contradictory evidence renders some assertion unwarranted.[37]

What is on the horizons of consciousness is ordered by its typical-

ity into what could be referred to as systems. These systems of typifications serve as a background against which the thematic kernels
of our attentional ray stand out. Objects come to our attention as
problematic because they violate the typicality expected of them.
"As long as the expectations adherent to the familiar knowledge continue to be fulfilled by the typicality of supervening experiences of
the same or similar objects, as long as the world will go on as antici-
pated in the stock of knowledge (i.e., of sedimented typifications),"
said Schutz, "we will acquiesce with the state of affairs."[38] As Dewey
might say it, something is problematic and thus "an object of
attentive regard," if it fails to achieve some measure of correspondence with that habitually expected.[39] Dewey would call typification
a form of habit which runs pre-reflectively until it is "impeded."[40]
When habit is violated, a tensed field is set up between what is
expected and what is perceived. It is this tension which brings the
violating object into consciousness as thematic. As Dewey put it,
"The homogeneity of qualitative relationships, *in the pro thought
material*, gives the tools or instruments by which thought is enabled
successfully to tackle the heterogeneity of collocations and conjunc-
tions also found in the same material." (Dewey's italics.)[41]

When Dewey identified mind as "the presence and operation of
meanings and ideas," he was referring to systems of typification or
what he called a "system of meanings."[42] (In a certain sense, Dewey's
conception of mind is quite similar to what Mead called the "me.")
According to Dewey, these meaning systems consist of habits which
amount to "unconscious expectation[s]" or meanings "organized in
certain channels." The mind, then, is a system of "predisposition[s]"
or "readiness[es] to act."[43] As Schutz puts it, "Typicality refers to
the set of expectations that future experiences will reveal these and
those typical traits to the same degree of anonymity and concrete-
ness. These expectations are merely another way of expressing the
general idealizations of 'and so forth and so on' and 'I can do it
again,' constitutive for the natural attitude."[44]

Neither Dewey nor Schutz meant to imply that habit originated
only in repetition. "Repetition," Dewey said, "is in no sense the essence of habit. Tendency to repeat acts is an incident of many habits
but not of all. The essence of habit is an acquired predisposition to
ways or modes of response, not to particular acts except as, under
special conditions, these express a way of behaving. Habit means

special sensitiveness or accessibility to certain classes of stimuli, standing predilections and aversions, rather than bare recurrence of specific acts."[45]

Habits constitute a "realm of things taken for granted," said Schutz.[46] They work quite automatically and, as Dewey put it, "by themselves are too organized, too insistent and determinate to need to indulge in inquiry or imagination. Habit as such is too definitely adapted to an environment to survey or analyze it. . . . Habit incorporates, enacts or overrides objects. . . ."[47] It is only when habits are impeded, when recipes fail, that consciousness is brought into play to restore continuity. Life is marked by a rhythm of interruption in, and recoveries of, the harmony characterizing our unimpeded habits. This fact explains James's celebrated contention that life is punctuated by a series of flights and perchings, or as Dewey phrased it, "interruption and reorganization."[48] Dewey contends that habits identify objects according to typicality and identify problems by separating the problematic from the background against which they appear.

Schutz makes the same case when he says that subjective familiarity has two meanings. It "refers on the one hand to the habits of the subject in recognizing, identifying and choosing actual experiences under the type at hand in his actual stock of knowledge. These habits in turn are not only the outcome of the object's personal history, the sedimentation of which they are, but also a function of his actual circumstances, the situational setting within which these habits have been formed. . . . On the other hand, the subjective meaning of familiarity refers to . . . the demarcation line which the subject draws between that segment of the world which needs and that which does not need further investigation."[49]

Typification is possible because man is a symbol-using animal, capable of learning and extending language. The importance of language in human affairs and the analysis of its function by Dewey and Schutz are topics worthy of separate study beyond the scope here. But it should be suggested that the field theory of consciousness and the closely allied theory of typification rest on and complement the possibility of language and communication.

Language is more than a mere labeling process. It allows man to detach meanings from the events which generated them. As Dewey put it, "Events turn into objects, things with meaning."[50] They have a unique quality, but at the same time unite with other acts of the same type. This amounts to what Schutz called a "gathering of separate Acts into a higher synthesis. This synthesis then becomes an 'object' within consciousness."[51] This phenomenon is significant, because it enables man to transcend the physical and temporal boundaries of the here and now.[52] Meanings can become "operative among things distant in space and time, through vicarious presence in a new medium."[53]

Meanings when separated from events do not float aimlessly in consciousness, lighting merely by chance on new situations. "By naming an experienced object," Schutz contended, "we are relating it by its typicality to preexperienced things of similar typical structure. . . ."[54] Dewey said, "Signs not only mark off specific and individual meanings, but they are also instruments of grouping meanings in relation to one another."[55]

Separating meaning from the occurrence of its conception is the central mechanism of the human mind. It enables man to accumulate experiences in order to develop self hood and accomplish self externalization. Berger has termed this an "ongoing outpouring of human being into the world."[56] This outpouring is achieved largely by communication, both internal and external. Typification and communication, then, work simultaneously. They serve the dialectically related aspects of human being—*homo externus* and *homo internus*—and make meaningful human action possible. It is little wonder that Dewey said, "Of all affairs, communication is the most wonderful." Events or objects typified in language receive "communicable meaning," said Dewey. "They have marks, notations, and are capable of con-notation and de-notation. They [become] more than mere occurrences, they have implications. Hence inference and reasoning are possible. . . ."[57] Schutz made a similar point when he said, "Any process of ratiocination presupposes language. . . ."[58] Once established, meanings can be carried in mind, put into ever larger and more varied contexts, and most wondrous of all, can be communicated to our fellow men.[59]

Language allows man a measure of liberation from the immediate. It gives him a heightened, if limited, control over his future. In choosing among courses of action, man can refer to his past experience and thereby "weigh his chances" in a fantasized future.[60] Dewey said that language and typification make it possible for "every experience [to live] on in future experiences" and for the past "[to] provide the only means . . . for understanding the present."[61] These

ideas, shared by Dewey and Schutz, are summarized poetically by
T. S. Eliot in "Burnt Norton":

> Time present and time past
> Are both perhaps present in time future,
> And time future contained in time past.[62]

A second point can be made about the liberating functions of language and typification. They allow us to transcend the boundaries
of the immediate and brute-given, and they provide us with possibilities for consciousness and for purposeful action. But simultaneously they bind us elastically to the past. The meanings which
language detaches from events assume a facticity which exists in consciousness, influencing, Dewey said, "the objective conditions under
which future experiences are had."[63] Man's externalizations can be
objectified. They cannot be wished away, nor can they be understood by others through mere introspection. If the past is always with
us, it is with us only by virtue of objectification. In Dewey's words,
things "discriminized and identified . . . are then 'objectified.' "[64]
Once established, objectifications or meanings are, Dewey said, self-
moving. As Berger and Luckmann have put it, they "carry within
them a tendency to persist."[65] When held in common by men, these
meanings have coercive power and a resistance just as forceful as
material objects. Dewey referred to these inter-subjective meanings
as embodying "essences which are as objective and coercive with
respect to opinions, emotions and sensations of individuals as are
physical objects. . . ." This led him to contend that the human power
to socially construct reality is both "liberating and regulating."[66] It
liberates in the sense of allowing men consciousness and control over
their lives. It regulates by necessarily narrowing the things of human
perception, prefiguring them into preexisting typification structures
which are changeable but nevertheless resist change.

SUBJECT-OBJECT UNIFICATION IN SITUATION

Nothing said so far was intended to suggest that subjective and objective elements are clearly divided in consciousness. Husserlian student Ludwig Binswanger said that such dualistic assumptions are the
"cancer of philosophy and psychology."[67] Dewey claimed these dual-
isms as "inward laceration[s]."[68] He termed them "arbitrary" and
the "acme of incredibility." For him, there was no "hard and fast

wall between the experiencing subject and that nature which is experienced."[69] Thus, when he spoke of experience, the term signified "the manifestation of interactions of organism and environment."[70] Experience, he said, "is not a veil that shuts man off from nature, it is a means of penetrating continually further into the heart of nature." One must keep in mind that "experience is *of* as well as *in* nature. It is not experience which is experienced, but nature. . . . Things interacting in certain ways *are* experience." (Dewey's italics.)[71]

Mind and nature influence mutually. Man does not strive merely to stencil "reality" on a *tabula rasa*. He acts to affect his environment, and he helps construct the world in which he externalizes his being.[72] The world is different by virtue of his existence, and he is different by virtue of the world. "Life goes on," Dewey said, "not merely in [an environment] but because of it, through interaction with it." Our organs of sense are not merely conduits bringing the external into the mind; they don't duplicate the world in a "Kodak fixation." Rather, they serve as "means of connection" between man and nature.[73] Dewey sees a fundamental error in trying to understand man's being-in-the-world by an exclusively subjective or objective analysis. We must "note that the adjusting is reciprocal; the brain not only enables organic activity to be brought to bear upon any object of the environment in response to a sensory stimulation, but this response also determines what the next stimulus will be."[74]

The reciprocity of man and environment can be illustrated by borrowing and embellishing an example first used by the Greek skeptic Carneades, and adapted by Alfred Schutz. He asks his readers to imagine a man who enters a room and notices something out of place. For our present purposes, let us assume the man enters a living room and finds a shirt cast carelessly in the corner. Schutz uses the example to ask why this shirt, of all the things potential to consciousness, is made the thematic kernel of the man's attentional ray. It is not enough to say the man chose to attend to the shirt: such explanations don't explain why that choice was made. Why is the shirt thematic, and not the clock, or the color of the shirt's buttons, or any of the myriad other objects in the room? To suggest that all by itself, the shirt called out for the man's attention is not convincing. Shirts, after all, don't always capture our attention and don't have intrinsic capacity to bring themselves into consciousness.

The phenomenon of the man's attending to the shirt makes sense only by accounting for the entire situation or, as Schutz put it, the "whole setting."[75] The man's expectations (typicality structures) were not violated solely by the shirt, but by its existence in the living room corner. Perhaps he would not have had the same reaction in a bedroom, tailor shop, or Chinese laundry. (A man with different experiences and typicality structures might not have seen the shirt.) The combination of man, living room, and shirt called out for the man's attention.

No single element of the situation explains the workings of the man's consciousness. The situation as a whole is grasped pre-reflectively by the man in question. His sedimented stock of knowledge forms the subjective aspects of the situation. The shirt, as it is placed in the living room, constitutes the most obvious objective element. They unite to form the "problem" in consciousness. It would make no sense to say that the shirt or consciousness were problematic in themselves. To use Dewey's language, the entire situation is inherently problematic, uncertain, unsettled, or disturbed.[76]

To explain experience fully, we cannot appeal merely to subjective elements of a situation. "The habit of disposing of the doubtful as if it belonged only to us rather than to the existential situation in which we are caught," said Dewey, "[is an unfortunate] inheritance from subjectivistic psychology."[77] Of course this does not view the subjective elements as impotent or nonexistent. It only means, as Schutz said, that "the activities of consciousness . . . take place within a very restricted scope of discretion."[78] To reconstruct a paradox alluded to earlier, Dewey claimed that these restrictions are "an indispensable condition of any human freedom."[79] Thus, when Schutz criticizes Sartre for his "contention that man is at every moment and in every circumstance free to make thematic whatever experience he pleases" without regard to the situation, he does so not in the spirit of denying subjective freedom, but in the hope of depicting more accurately where and under which conditions freedom can be said to exist.[80]

On the other side of the issue, the purely objectivistic explanations of the man's attention are found to be as insufficient as the solely subjectivistic ones. It is erroneous to believe that the shirt is attended to because it is a stimulus the man cannot resist and one to which he can only adjust. Dewey pointed to this error in his famous answer to Watsonian stimulus-response psychology, "The Reflex Arc Concept in Psychology." A stimulus is a "conscious fact," insisted Dewey, and cannot be treated "as a mere physical event."[81] The shirt in the corner did not stimulate attention; the shirt as constituted (interpreted) in consciousness accounted for the man's interest. A stimulus and a response, then, are not "distinct mental existences" but are found "in reality . . . always inside a coordination."[82] To separate them is to miss the circuitry of unified experience.

Schutz argued against the same form of behaviorism when he noted that the organism must indeed come to terms with its environment. However, said Schutz, "it would be a serious misunderstanding—but one which is common to much current psychology—to interpret this notion as a mere 'adjustment to the environment.'" For both Schutz and Dewey, environment was "not a sector of the world simply imposed upon us from the outside, something . . . with which we may come to terms only if we 'adjust' or 'adapt' ourselves to it. At best this is but an aspect of its meaning." Environment, Schutz insisted, has its subjective aspects and must be understood "as a whole" rather than dualistically.[83]

The conceptions of situation and interaction are inseparable. Interaction, said Dewey, "assigns equal rights to both factors in experiences—objective and internal conditions. Any normal experience is an interplay of these two sets of conditions. Taken together, or in their interaction, they form what we call a situation."[84] Problems are constructed in consciousness through an interaction of our stock of meanings and intentional objects. The indeterminate quality of a problem pervades the entire situation and is not formed solely by fiat of ego nor independently in nature. Rather, the whole situation is problematic. It is constituted in consciousness by a tensed transactional field developing through the interaction of objective and subjective elements of experience. The problem will not necessarily be "straightened out, cleared up or put in order," said Dewey, by mere "manipulation of our personal states of mind" or by passively awaiting changes in nature. Restoration of equilibrium "can be effected . . . only by operations which actually modify existing conditions" and thereby change the character or quality of the entire situation.[85]

Schutz makes a distinction between "working" and "performing." In the former, changes in the outer world are made by bodily movement; in the latter, no changes are brought about by physical action. Dewey would find this distinction unnecessary. According to his notion of situation, changes are made during both performance and working. For certain kinds of analysis, it may be useful heuristically to make such divisions between work and performance, but not for a full understanding of experience.

The previous paragraphs have risked repetition in order to avoid a narrowness of vision alive, if not dominant, within phenomenologically oriented sectors of social science. There are some who claim subjectivity is paramount in experience. At worst, this reification of man's capacity for externalization seems to ignore the existence of environment and its influence on human existence. Schutz's imaginative use of phenomenological philosophy clearly avoided the error of these latter-day subjectivists. As Natanson has pointed out, Schutz's "use of the term 'subjective' . . . refers to the fact that meaning is related to the experiencing individual, to the individual as a 'subject' of experience, and not to any private or idiosyncratic translation of experience which is limited to the individual and which may vary from person to person."[86] Thus, when Schutz asked social scientists "to deal with human conduct and its common-sense interpretation in . . . social reality," he said that "such an analysis refers by necessity to the subjective point of view."[87]

But Schutz did not mean this in any narrow sense. With Dewey, he believed that problematic situations grow from a transaction between man and nature and that situations are "constituted" in consciousness. Both men understood that the social sciences must penetrate the construction of the subjective point of view in order to understand human activity and being. They did not intend that the subjective be distinct and exclusive of those forces with which it constantly interacts. Nor did they wish to commit the identical error on the other side of the issue by reifying nature to the point where man's only function is to respond to, and come to terms with, imposing stimuli. "Situations," said Schutz, "if not of our own making [are] nevertheless of our definition, and such 'definition' is precisely the way in which we come to terms with [them]."[88] The error of emphasizing one phase of human experience to the elimination of the other has tended to divide behavioral scientists into warring camps of those who would study man through the functioning of his institutions (Durkheim, for example), and those who would focus on the meanings of interaction among individuals (Weber, for example). Such mutually exclusive categorizations, Dewey claimed, are about as reasonable "as a division of botanists into rootists and flowerists."[89]

6. The Problem of Relevance

Wᴵᴸᴸᴵᴀᴹ Jᴀᴍᴇs characterized consciousness as a series of perchings and flights. He meant that man does not live in a state of constant, animated consciousness. Life is not continually problematic. There are periods of rest, of perching between flights into problematic areas. Just as consciousness is launched from the sphere of the unproblematic, so must it return to the unity of that sphere. Therefore, an analysis of the unproblematic workings of the mind must be included in any consideration of the workings of consciousness as they deal with a problem.

The rhythm suggested by James's metaphor of flights and perchings is instructive, but it could be misleading. It would be easy to assume that the workings of the mind are as separate from the workings of consciousness as perching is from flight. Mind could be interpreted as a kind of dormant state disconnected totally from consciousness and of a different order. This would be a misunderstanding of human experience. The habitual mind is continually active, even as consciousness reigns. They are not foreign, but they complement each other in a way not suggested by James's metaphor. The horizons surrounding the thematic kernel in consciousness are supplied by the mind. In their totality, horizons constitute the mind.

This relationship between mind and consciousness has already been suggested in our discussion of consciousness as a field. It leads us toward other questions which the rest of this study will examine. In a situation where possibilities are open, where numerous things within an unstructured field are available to man's attention, how is he able to select certain facts as relevant and worthy of attention and to neglect others? As Schutz has said, it is a "question of why these facts and precisely these are selected . . . as relevant."[1] To attempt an answer, it is necessary to investigate how the unproblematic becomes problematic. The task then is to show how consciousness deals with a problem and to explain how the unproblematic aids in defining, as well as in solving, the problem at hand. It will be necessary to know how different forms of relevance serve consciousness at different stages of inquiry. Schutz's terminology will guide this analysis, but at each step we will see how Dewey's ideas complement or contradict those of Schutz.

The analysis will deal with three related but nonetheless distinct forms of relevance—motivational, thematic, and interpretive. Of these, motivational relevance is the most complicated and perhaps the most controversial.

MOTIVATIONAL RELEVANCE

INTEREST AS MOTIVE

Schutz contended that interest is the prime motive for human attention, the central force in the motility of consciousness. "The interest prevailing at the moment," he said, "determines the elements which an individual singles out of the surrounding objective world . . . so as to define his situation." Interest is a form of relevance which motivates an individual to be attentive to "this" object rather than to "that" object.[2] Schutz calls these interests our "motivational relevances" and explains they "are sedimentations of previous experiences . . . which [have] led to a permanent habitual possession of knowledge. . . ." The term "interest," says Schutz, "refers to a system of motivational relevances . . . which guide the selective activity of [the] mind."[3] To say we attend to something because it interests us is, on the face of it, to say very little indeed. It begs the question of why we want to attend to "this" rather than to "that."

A second and related problem found in the notion of interest as motive is the disturbingly subjective connotations of the word. Dewey used the word "interest" in ways very similar to Schutz. Nevertheless, he was aware of the problem of implied subjectivity. He once wrote to his friend and collaborator, Arthur Bentley, warning that "the words 'interest' [and] 'concern' are of course dangerous to use at present—they are too loaded with 'subjectivistic mentalism.' "[4]

Our shirt-in-the-corner example illustrates the problem to which Dewey referred. If we say the man attended to the shirt because it interested him, we risk suggesting that his attention is explained by a mere act of will. Schutz was making no such suggestion. While he argued against sociologists who fled all things subjective in their pursuit of objectivity, he nevertheless was aware that an analysis of the objective aspects of experience had its place in philosophy and the social sciences. He believed it important to acknowledge the subjective elements in man's construction of reality. But he did not assume that this construction occurred in total, free-wheeling fantasy unrelated to things external to consciousness. "The ontological structure of the universe is imposed upon me," Schutz wrote, "and constitutes the frame of all possible spontaneous activity. Within this frame, I have to find my bearings and I have to come to terms with its elements."[5]

What is the nature of the objective component of interest, or what Schutz preferred to call motivational relevance? To answer this, we need to look at the role played by objective components in Schutz's understanding of experience.

THE OBJECTIVE CONTRIBUTION

"Interest is itself . . . a function of situational circumstances," wrote Schutz. Situations, as we have discussed in an earlier section, have both subjective and objective components. Despite its implied subjectivism, interest, then, is formed in a union of subjective and objective components and does not exist independently in either. This point is found in Schutz's contention that objects can "impose themselves upon my attention." Rather than my simply being interested in them, "they interest me."[6] He refers to this form of interest as "imposed motivational relevance" and through the use of this concept grants that there are limits (sometimes quite severe) to the spontaneity of attention.

Interest is the product of situations, and funded by varying degrees of volition. In some cases, the volitional aspects of the situation seem minimal: these situations, said Schutz, are "not . . . particularly voluntary."[7] In contradistinction to these are situations initiated by a higher degree of volitional ego activity, those which are funded by more conscious volition. In those cases, Schutz refers to "intrinsic" or "volitional" relevance structures.

Man is born into a physical and cultural world with which he must come to terms. The objects of our environment have facticity and coercive power. As Dewey stated, "The object is that which objects."[8] (Dewey is very close in this contention to Max Scheler's notion of "resistance.") Because objects object, they can be said to impose themselves on us. The "human situation," said Dewey, "falls wholly within nature. It reflects the traits of nature; it gives indisputable evidence that in nature itself qualities and relations, individualities and uniformities, finalities and efficacies, contingencies and necessities are inexplicably bound together."[9] As Dewey said elsewhere, "Life goes on in an environment; not merely *in* it but because of it, through interaction with it." (Dewey's italics.) Without the resistance which the world surrounding him supplies, Dewey believed that man could not become aware of himself as "self," and that he would be without feeling or interest.[10] The things of nature are an indispensable part of man's world. To the extent that idealism neglects the impositional existence of nature, it fails to adequately account for the nature of human experience. Schutz's introduction of "imposed relevance" avoids the problem of "subjectivistic mentalism" which Dewey said is implied in the word "interest." Schutz grants the imposition of the "ontological structures" of nature which cannot be willed away and with which "I have to come to terms."[11]

However, the notion of imposed interest introduces new dangers. Implied subjectivism is now balanced by an implied objectivism. The latter suggests that objects of the world have power to introduce themselves into consciousness, to chisel themselves upon the *tabula rasa*. There is reason to question whether it is possible to solve the errors of subjectivistic idealism by introducing the equivalent errors of objectivistic realism. On the surface, Schutz seems to have done this by balancing the apparently contradictory notions of imposition and interest. But he has opened himself to a criticism no less troublesome than those arising from his use of the term "interest." Dewey puts this type of criticism quite clearly. "It is frequently said to be the object which attracts attention, which calls forth interest to itself by its own inherent qualities. But this is a psychological impossibility."[12] Schutz was not guilty of this error, although his use of language suggests he might be. Therefore, we must look more carefully at his idea of imposed relevance.

Schutz did not intend to join the philosophical camp of the realists by using the term "imposed relevance." The word "imposed" does not refer to the workings of the experienced objects, and it does not impute to them any power greater than mere existence. "Imposed" is meant to be descriptive of the subjective, pre-reflective interpretation of the experiencing agent. It describes the "having" of the experience and not its funding processes. It is descriptive of the "lived experience" and not of experience formation. Schutz uses the term "motivational relevancy," because "it is . . . experienced as a motive for the definition of the situation."[13] His analysis of the situational character of the human experience parallels Dewey's. But unlike Dewey, he chooses language which is not descriptive of the working components of the situation but rather of the subjective experiencing of those components. Thus, when he says that an object "interests me" or "imposes itself upon me," he is not speaking of some intentional power within the object but rather of the experiencing of the object by the subject. Because objects "may be experienced as imposed from without," Schutz introduces the term "imposed relevance."[14]

We shall see in greater detail that interest is established in a union of self and object. The contributions of the self are made by sedimented past experiences which live on in man as habits. Contributions from these habits in the formation of interest may not seem to come from the self because they are produced by a self not consciously known. Because interest is experienced as imposed, it is often attributed to some outside force. On this point, Dewey and Schutz are remarkably close in analysis. The implications of habit in experience will be examined further in the section on the pre-reflective union of subject and object.

Schutz's analysis of human experience contains a recognition of objective forces. This recognition was not simply a balancing of the errors of idealism and realism. Rather, it was a recognition that situations compel action.[15] And situations are made of subjective and objective factors. If his language suggests a dualism, it is only because a dualism suggests itself in the consciousness of the experiencing subject and not because it exists in fact.

THE SUBJECTIVE CONTRIBUTION

If what Schutz says is true, that objects of the world play a part through the sheer power of their existence in funding our motives, then what part does man play? Are man's interests mere stencilings of his environment? To answer these questions, it might help to refer to a distinction which Schutz draws between types of motives—the "because" and the "in-order-to."

As man lives in his on-going actions, his perspective is limited to what Dewey referred to as the man's "ends-in-view." If we ask a person in the course of some action what motivates that action, his answer is likely to be in terms of his future purpose: "I work hard in order to get ahead." In this example of a typical end-in-view defini-

tion of motivation, the motive is future-directed. The action is purposeful and its motive defined in terms of its purpose. Schutz refers
to this motive as of the "in-order-to" type. It is the motive as it is
subjectively experienced by the actor. "Motive means [to the man]
what he has actually in view as bestowing meaning upon his ongoing
action, and this is always the in-order-to motive. . . ."[16] This is an
important motive and worthy of careful study, but it does not exhaust the human input to situations. An adequate theory of motivation must go further. It requires "an analysis of the underlying
systems of relevancy," said Schutz. Without such an analysis, "no
foundation of a science of human action is possible."[17]

Man need not limit his perspective to motivations of the "in-order-
to" variety. As Dewey and Schutz like to put it, he can "stop and
think."[18] He can probe the "underlying systems of relevancy" which
fund his actions with meanings but yet are not consciously present
as he acts. It is only when action has been halted, Schutz observed,
that a man "may turn back to his past action as an observer of himself and investigate by what circumstances he has been determined
to do what he did."[19] The motives revealed in this act of reflection
differ from the "in-order-to" variety. The latter is on-going and
available to man in his lived acts. The former demands this future-
oriented action stop; it has to be reconstructed from completed
actions in the past. This reconstruction seeks out the "lived experience temporally prior to the project" in question and which motivates
it.[20] We refer to "in-order-to motives" in terms of future time but to
"because-motives" in the pluperfect tense.

"Because-motives" invariably refer back to the stock of knowledge
at hand. For example, we can say that the man in the shirt-in-the-
corner situation investigated the shirt to find out what it was doing
in his living room. But to answer why he attended to the shirt in the
first place, we must refer to the "because-motives" formed from past
experience: they automatically informed him that the shirt violated
the typicality of the living room. Sedimented past experiences form
the habits which fund consciousness, and "because-motives" refer to
those habits which are at work pre-reflectively in experience.

Neither type of motivation springs from man's spontaneous ego,
totally unaffected by the ontological structures of the world. Interest
has no existence prior to objects. It does not exist in some hermeti-
cally sealed state of privacy within the mind, poised to latch onto
free-floating objects of the world. The most we can say is that habits

are expectancies. Dewey put it more precisely: "Every habit creates an unconscious expectation. It forms a certain outlook."[21]

Habits which are not actively funding consciousness are too anonymous to be interests. Interests are habits at work, not habits at rest. Like consciousness itself, interest does not exist prior to union with objects of the environment. Just as phenomenologists insist there is no such thing as pure consciousness but always consciousness of something, so it must be said that interest is not a pure state of mind but always intends an object. One is not simply interested, he is interested *in something*. Interests are not pure attitudes, said Dewey, but "always attitudes toward objects."[22]

Interest has subjective aspects. Dewey noted that it can be "active, projective, and propulsive." It can strive for an end-in-view. Further, it can signify "an *internal* realization, or feeling, of worth." In short, interest has its emotional and active sides, as well as its objective ones. Dewey offered an inkling of this in the etymology of the word "interest." *Inter-esse*, "to be between," suggests that interest is formed in a transaction between subject and object, between internal habits and the existential things of the situation. "Interest marks the annihilation of the distance between subject and object," said Dewey. "It is the instrument which effects their organic union."[23]

Individuals may enter a situation in various ways. When one begins to think, Dewey said, "he does not leave his characteristic affection[s] behind." Thus, an aspect of any context must be what Dewey called "selective interest," a term paralleling closely what Schutz means by "because-motives." In words very close to those of Schutz, Dewey explains, "Every particular case of thinking is what it is because of some attitude, some bias if you will. . . . This attitude is no immediate part of what is consciously reflected upon, but it determines the selection of this rather than that subject matter. . . . There is selectivity (and rejection) found in every operation of thought." Selective interest is not in itself subject matter, as we have already suggested, but is "a mode of selection that determines subject matter" in consciousness.[24]

We have already indicated that Schutz's "in-order-to" motives parallel Dewey's conception of an action's end-in-view. Schutz's "because-motives" coincide to a great degree with Dewey's conception of selective interest (habit) working at the pre-reflective levels of consciousness. This point is elaborated further in the section on the pre-reflective union of subject and object. In anticipation of that, some concluding points should be made concerning motivational relevances. James seems to have been very close to the concept of motivational relevance when he wrote in 1890:

> Passive sensoral attention is *derived* when the impression, without being either strong or of an instinctively exciting nature, is connected by previous experience and education with things that are so. These things may be called the *motives* of the attention. The impression draws an interest from them. . . ; the result is that it is brought into the focus of the mind. [James's italics.][25]

These words serve nicely as a review of points covered so far in this section. James states that attention is derived from previous experience. The mind selects the objects of its attention, but selection is accomplished by what James called a connection of object and subject. We receive objects as sensory impressions; they are given meaning as they unite with habits formed by our previous experiences. Dewey referred to this transactional melding as an "organic union." The word "organic" emphasizes the reciprocity of the dialectic involvement of subject and object. Schutz makes the same point by referring to the phenomenon as a synthesis. It makes sense, then, for him to say that "motivational relevances are sedimentations of previous experience" which have been raised to consciousness by sensory perceptions.[26]

Interest derives from the interpenetration of subject and object. The interests awakened by an object of attention are dormantly present "as habitual possessions of my stock of knowledge," said Schutz. Habit is transformed into interest through a pre-reflective union of object and habit. Thus, Schutz saw "interest as originating in motivational relevances . . . ."[27] To understand an interest as it motivates man to action, it is necessary to seek the "lived experience temporally prior to the project," which is the "because-motive" of that action.[28] This brings us to the heart of Schutz's sociology. Social scientists cannot understand any human action without first reducing it to the situation where it develops and referring it to the motives present there. As Schutz put it, "Social things are only understandable if they can be reduced to human activities; and human activities are only made understandable by showing their in-order-to or because motives."[29] These ideas are reminiscent of Dewey's concern for a "psychological method for sociology" which he voiced in his essay on the savage mind. They bring us to a consideration of the pre-reflective sphere of human experience.

THE PRE-REFLECTIVE UNION OF
SUBJECT AND OBJECT

In his everyday activities, an individual is guided by conditions of the world outside himself and the "terminated experiences" which have sedimented in memory according to various habitual systems of typicality.[30] These systems are taken for granted within the natural attitude of daily life, until intervening forces prove them to be problematic. As Schutz explained, we live by the tacit "assumption that what has proved valid thus far in our experience will remain valid in the future [and] that what thus far I have been able to accomplish in the world by acting upon it I shall be able to accomplish again and again in the future."[31]

Human experience is accomplished through union of sedimented habit and worldly objects. What then is to be said of will? Where is the spontaneity which Schutz claimed existed in the workings of intrinsic (volitional) motivational relevances? Such questions lead us to consider the importance of habit and to re-examine Schutz's notion of imposed or intrinsic relevance.

Schutz contended that interest was of two types: imposed or intrinsic. We have already tried to show that in all cases interest results from an "organic union" of self and object. However, we have acknowledged that Schutz's distinction between imposed and intrinsic relevance is correct only if it describes how the union is experienced by the subject ("lived," "had," or "felt"), rather than describing widely divergent processes of interest formation. How these types of interest involve human will must be shown now.

Schutz said that imposed interests (motivational relevances of the "because" variety) are formed by "passive synthesis."[32] This is "not a particularly voluntary act," but one in which objects of the world "awaken" expectancies of habit. According to Schutz's analysis, we are habitually receptive to objects which are "passively pre-given" to consciousness as typical of objects of past experience. This form of human receptivity represents "the lowest form of ego activity."[33] Objects of the world are appropriated without necessity of conscious intention. "This appropriation takes place," according to Schutz, "not by acts of logical judgment but according to a certain *typicalness* of the appropriated object, by reason of which it is experienced as being in relation . . . with other objects of the same familiar type. . . ." (Schutz's italics.)[34]

The level of ego activity fluctuates according to our degree of familiarity with some portion of our stock of knowledge and how closely the intended object corresponds to what is expected of it. The least amount of ego is involved, Schutz said, in "our *routine actions* in daily life, . . . the manifold chores" which are performed automatically "according to recipes which were learned and have been practiced with success thus far." (Schutz's italics.) In these cases, "we follow our routines . . . as a matter of course so long as nothing interferes which might hamper the normal (that is, the unquestioned and hitherto efficient) process of our ongoing activities."[35] These daily activities demand little or no reflective thought. They are performed unconsciously, if we take this word without its Freudian connotations. Ego activity of a higher level occurs when routine activities have become problematic for any one of numerous reasons. In such cases, man can rely no longer on routine and must seek a new harmony with his surroundings.

Schutz insisted that routine, unproblematic activities are funded by motivational relevances which are taken for granted. When the routine is broken in some way, this violation is registered pre-reflectively. It occurs in the "pre-predicative sphere" where objects are spontaneously perceived by consciousness as problematic. Violations come to mind, said Schutz, "whether or not we want them to do so."[36] They don't seem to be consciously intended, nor are they experienced as being brought to our attention willfully. This is what Schutz meant by saying the process involves a low level of ego activity. But does this mean that human will has nothing to do with human perception?

It is necessary to make certain distinctions in order to answer this. In routine acts, our recognitions are automatic. They are funded by past experiences which have become taken for granted as reliable. Dewey claimed that in these mere recognitions, "we fall back, as upon a stereotype, upon some previously formed scheme. Some detail or arrangement of details serves as a cue for bare identification. It suffices in recognition to apply this bare outline as a stencil to the present object."[37] Dewey acknowledges another form of recognition, a higher order which he calls "perception." He insisted that the two differ immensely.

> Recognition is perception arrested before it has a chance to develop freely. In recognition there is a beginning of an act of perception. But this beginning is not allowed to serve the development of a full perception of the thing recognized. It is arrested at the point where *it will serve some other purpose*, as

when we recognize a man on the street in order to greet or avoid him, not so as to see him for the sake of seeing what is there. [Italics added.][38]

Recognition is the automatic, pre-reflective result of habits at work. But habits are not as passive as Schutz's language would suggest. This point is important to the question of will. "All habits," said Dewey, "are demands for certain kinds of activity. . . . In any intelligible sense of the word 'will,' they *are* will. They form our effective desires and they furnish us with our working capacities. They rule our thoughts, determining which shall appear and be strong and which shall pass from light into obscurity." (Dewey's italics.)[39] Elaborating further in *Democracy and Education*, Dewey said: "Any habit marks an *inclination*—an active preference and choice for the conditions involved in its exercise. A habit does not wait, Micawber-like, for a stimulus to turn up so that it may get busy; it actively seeks occasions to pass into full operation." (Dewey's italics.)[40]

Thus, it is possible to conclude that human will is active even at the most routine level of activity—that of pre-problematic recognition which Schutz and Husserl unfortunately have called "passive synthesis." Schutz is correct that there are higher levels of volition possible than those at work in unencumbered, habitual activity. Habit may be exposed to, and extended by, reflective thought "for the sake of seeing what is there." Perception can replace bare recognition. When this is accomplished, said Dewey, "consciousness becomes fresh and alive."[41] This ego activity, Schutz contends, *is* thus of a higher order. The motivational relevance at work is no longer imposed; it is intrinsic to the situation itself and earns Schutz's label of "intrinsic motivational relevance."

Simple recognition (a re-cognizing of past experience) occurs outside imposed routines "in order to" accomplish some end external to itself. The definition as it applies to the elements within a situation is superficial and is funded by an already established "end-in-view." But habits need not be so superficially accepted. That which "is directly and nonreflectively experienced," Dewey said, can be transformed into "an object of thought for the sake of its own development. . . ."[42] In such cases, our "attention is redirected" from some extrinsic end-in-view to intentional objects alive within the situation. The motivation springs now from sources closer to the situation and does not lie in thoughtless routine. Perception no longer services routine but is directed toward "this individual thing existing here and now with all the unrepeatable particularities that accompany and mark such existences." Thus, Dewey claimed, there is an "expanding [of] the significance of the object." The process, of course, presupposes the pre-reflective workings which brought the object to recognition in the first place. But it transcends this immediacy and requires time for its own development. Dewey put it succinctly. "In no case can there be *perception of an object* except in a process developing in time. Mere excitation, yes; but not an object perceived, instead of just recognized as one of a familiar kind." (Dewey's italics.)[43]

The important distinctions to be made are not between experiences which contain human volition and those which do not. Even when habits are working pre-reflectively, they constitute human will; therefore, such distinctions are impossible. This was Dewey's point when he said, "No experience having a meaning is possible without some element of thought." Thus, the only helpful distinction is made "according to the proportion of reflection found" in experience.[44] In effect, this is the distinction Schutz has made between intrinsic and imposed relevances. The former involves a higher component of reflective thought than the latter, which does not extend beyond the pre-reflective workings of habit. If my interpretation is correct, it seriously challenges the definition Helmet Wagner offered in a glossary to Schutz's terminology. Wagner wrote: "Insofar as relevances spring from a person's own interests and motivations, they are *volitional*. If they are urged upon him either by situational conditions or by social imposition, they are *imposed*." (Wagner's italics.)[45] As I have tried to show, such a definition makes little sense. No interest can exist outside a situation; thus, it cannot be "owned" in any purely subjective sense. *All interests are situational.* The only distinctions worth making are among the amounts of reflective activity funding a particular interest.

We are now closer to the phenomenon of man's motile impulses as a choice-making being. We are better prepared perhaps to examine the subjective vitality of human action and to attempt to account for what Maurice Natanson called the "nisus of consciousness."[46] Schutz attempted to explain man's motile impulses by examining the workings of relevance. But the phenomenon of relevance is explainable only within the context of situations, and this is the thrust of our argument. Further, any appeal to some "fundamental" state of man's "being-in-the-world," which attempts to find the nexus of relevance or its primal groundings, is unnecessary.

Much of what has been said so far about the field of consciousness, subject-object unification in situation, and the concept of typification, is in an effort to point out the importance of the pre-reflective in human experience. It is within the pre-reflective sphere that situations are constituted. However, it is very difficult to penetrate the pre-reflective sphere or to examine situations as they fund experience. This is because a "situation as such is not and cannot be stated or made explicit. It is taken for granted," said Dewey, " 'understood,' or implicit, in all propositional symbolization. It forms the universe of discourse" and cannot be made available within that discourse as an intentional object. To make it an intentional object and thus available to reflection, is to place it within a new context, a new situation, which again is not observable in its silent and anonymous functioning. Dewey is careful to clarify his language. When he says that a situation is "implicit" in all that transpires within an experience, he "does not signify that it is implied. It is present throughout as that of which whatever is explicitly stated or propounded is a distinction."[47] In this rather awkward sentence, Dewey is saying that whatever becomes explicit within the situation does so as a distinction of that situation. The situation is alive as a quality within all its components, and its parts derive meaning and force in consciousness by virtue of the situation in which they appear.

Natanson has briefly and perhaps tentatively proposed that the problem of relevance is grounded in man's most basic experience, the lurking anticipation of death.[48] To support this claim, he refers to an interesting passage from Schutz's essay, "On Multiple Realities."

> The whole system of relevances which governs us within the natural attitude is founded upon the basic experience of each of us: I know that I shall die and I fear to die. This basic experience we suggest calling the *fundamental anxiety*. It is the primordial anticipation from which all the others originate. From the fundamental anxiety spring the many interrelated systems of hopes and fears . . . which incite man within the natural attitude to attempt the mastery of the world, to overcome obstacles, to draft projects, and to realize them. [Schutz's italics.][49]

Natanson's analysis tries to move the focus of phenomenology back to the most "fundamental," "basic," "primordial" experience of human existence and in so doing to identify that experience as the "taproot of the problem" of relevance.[50] The accuracy of this identification does not concern us here, although the topic is interesting. (Dewey might not argue this proposition. It seems compatible with his naturalistic concerns for the vegetative aspects of survival.) Our purposes are accomplished if we show that even the most primordial of man's experiences, as identified by Schutz, can only be understood contextually, that is, within situation.

Despite its fundamental nature, the anxiety of which Schutz speaks is not a pure state of consciousness. "When it is said that I have a feeling," Dewey observed, "what is actually designated is primarily the presence of a dominating quality in a situation as a whole, not just the existence of a feeling as a psychical or psychological fact."[51] The feeling of anxiety pervading the realization of human mortality presumably is not an inborn trait but is acquired in the process of living. Like all other emotions, it is intentional and occurs within a field. Emotions, said Calvin Schrag, "are not isolated and incapsulated psychic states."[52] Anxiety is an emotion. As such, Dewey insists, it must be "attached to events." Emotions, he said, are like interests: "They are not, save in pathological instances, private."[53] They grow in the transactional nexus of self and object.

From this observation, Dewey moved directly to the problem of relevance. "Emotion is the moving and cementing force. It selects what is congruous and dyes what is selected with its color, thereby giving qualitative unity to materials externally disparate and dissimilar. It thus provides unity in and through the varied parts of an experience."[54] Emotion, then, *is the felt quality of the situation*, the lived experience of the subject within the situation. It is the quality binding the situation into an organic unit and serving, Schrag observed, "as a mode of entry into the world." Through its auspices, "dimensions of the world *as I exist in it* are uncovered and brought to light." (Schrag's italics.)[55] The qualitative unity of the situation accounts for relevance.

Dewey observed that this "underlying unity of qualitativeness *regulates pertinence or relevancy.* . . . It guides selection and rejection and the manner of utilization of all explicit terms." (Italics added.) The quality of a situation is not an object of our awareness "by itself but [is only known] as the background, the thread, and the directive clue in what we do expressly think of. For the latter things are *its* distinctions and relations." (Dewey's italics.) It is interesting to note that Dewey footnotes a dissatisfaction with James's use of the term "fringes" at this point, "because the metaphor tends to treat [the qualitative character of situation] as an additional element instead of an all-pervasive influence in determining contents."[56]

For Dewey, then, the qualitative character of a situation is the taproot of relevancy and not a single "primordial" or "most fundamental" quality, i.e., the anxiety accompanying the recognition of death. The anxiety of death is itself a quality. Although a profound one, it is formed in the same way as all other emotional qualities, within situation. The recognition of death is a pervasive influence on man's actions. Berger observed that "legitimations of the reality of the social world *in the face of death* are decisive requirements in any society." (Berger's italics.)[57] But this says only that the "fundamental anxiety" is a quality of such force and so universally characteristic of man, that it is an influence in many human situations.[58] But it is a quality, and as such is situational in character. It qualifies all that falls within its situational domain, and that domain, in the case of the "fundamental anxiety," may be very wide indeed.

Victor Kestenbaum has pointed out that interpreters of Dewey's philosophy have overlooked too frequently his use of habit in his notion of experience. One result has been an incomplete understanding of Dewey's notion of the qualitative in experience. Kestenbaum argues persuasively that "the qualitative is ultimately a function of the habitual."[59] The quality of a situation is "immediately felt," said Dewey, and is therefore not the result of conscious reflection. In so arguing, Dewey approaches "Bergson's contention that intuition precedes conception. . . . Reflection and rational elaboration spring from and make explicit a prior intuition."[60] Intuition (the immediate lived experience) forms the platform from which the "rational elaboration" springs; it is the "directly experienced quality" which is "present and prior to and independent of all reflective analysis." This "immediately felt" lived experience is intuitive but is not simply a psychic state. Rather, it results from a union of the tendentious, habitual self and the surrounding world. Intentional habits form an organic union with intended objects. The result is an immediately felt "underlying quality which operates to control" subsequent conscious actions. The underlying quality of which Dewey speaks seems equivalent to Schutz's notion of motivational relevance. This relevance or quality accounts for the motility of choice between contending objects and must be seen as the backbone of thought itself.

"The immediate existence of quality," Dewey said, "is the background, the point of departure and the regulative principle of all thinking."[61]

Man perceives objects through his sensory apparatuses. But it is through the apparatus of habit, or as Schutz called it, "passive or automatic, habitual knowledge," that sensory impressions receive meaning.[62] This temporal synthesis of past meaning and present circumstances renders the static perceptions dynamic and meaningful. And this melding of meaning and circumstance gives situations their qualitative dimension. "By some physiological process, not exactly understood at present but to which the name 'habit' is given," Dewey said, "the net outcome of prior experiences gives a dominant quality, designated 'promontory' to a perceived existence."[63]

Dewey insisted that it is "through habits formed in intercourse with the world," that man is able to "in-habit the world." Because of habit, he does not approach the world "with an empty mind." He comes upon each moment of life "with a background of experiences long ago funded into capacities and likes or with a commotion due to more recent experiences. He comes with a mind waiting, patient, willing to be impressed and yet not without bias and tendency. . . ."[64] Habits are motile and the foundation of consciousness. Within the natural attitude, said Dewey, "habit assumes the essential likeness of the new situation with the old." Habit works within this attitude pre-reflectively, routinely, below the level of conscious intention. The habitual serves as a mode "of preference and esteem."[65] It not only brings objects into consciousness with funded meanings but concurrently and pre-reflectively assigns them what phenomenologists have called a "wait." This wait can refer to likelihood or value or degree of individual interest in the intended object.[66]

It can be argued further that habits allow man to work simultaneously at various levels of conscious intention. For example, Schutz suggested that the act of writing a theoretical paper entails a variety of activities "spread over several realms or levels of my conscious life." Ego is habitually peripheral to the act of writing; the formation of what is to be said, the theoretical work, is the focus of thematic regard. These different activities are joined in a single tension of consciousness and are lived simultaneously. "It is the predominance of the theme which creates the apparent unification of this set of activities, and it bestows the main accent of reality upon the realm of theoretical contemplation. Seen from this perspective all the other activities simultaneously performed in other dimensions seem to be not irreal but subordinate and ancillary." The thematic kernel is paramount in consciousness and is surrounded by other provinces of meaning which operate below the level of conscious attention. These separate yet unified activities "put into play various levels of our personality."[67] Some demand the highest tension of consciousness, while others work subconsciously. The significant point is that they are held together by a single, qualitative tension, understood only when the whole situation is taken into account.

The nature of Schutz's examples suggests physical habits which can be performed so automatically they need little or no conscious thought. The act of writing proceeds unproblematically and therefore does not interfere with the paramount theme of creative thought.[68] What is true for the physical habit of writing is true also for nonphysical habits. Mental habits operate on the horizons of consciousness. They form what Dewey calls the system of meaning, and they constitute mind. Thus, "The greater part of mind is only implicit in any conscious act or state; the field of mind—of operative meanings—is enormously wider than that of consciousness."[69]

Habits are man's scheme of reference. "All interpretation of [the world of daily life] is based," said Schutz, "upon a stock of previous experiences of it, our own experiences and those handed down to us by [others], which in the form of 'knowledge at hand' function as a scheme of reference."[70] The organic union of habit and world resulting in a qualitative situation cannot be interpreted as mere coincidence or a tying together of essentially separate entities. Quality is more than the result of reflectively matching things past with things present. "An experience is always what it is," Dewey said, "because of the transaction taking place between an individual and what, at the time, constitutes his environment. . . ."[71] This transaction forms the predominant quality of the situation and accounts for relevancy, interest, and emotion.

The importance of the word "transaction" cannot be overestimated. It does not suggest a simple association of likenesses between things remembered and things perceived. Rather, it demands "a fusion so complete as to incorporate both members into a single whole." The "expressiveness of an object" (that which is intrinsic within its own ontological structure) has a force to which the observing self must, in a sense, yield. The perceiving subject must be impressionable before he can be impressed. But, Dewey reiterates, the subject does not approach the world with an empty mind, and this fact enables objects to be expressive. An object's mere being is not expressive in itself. Speaking about works of art, Dewey said, "The other factor that is required in order that a work may be expressive to a percipient is meanings and values extracted from prior experiences and funded in such a way that they fuse with the qualities directly presented in the work of art."[72]

Kestenbaum explains the transactional nature of the constituting act of perception in this way:

> What Dewey is attempting to do in arguing that past meanings and present qualities form an "internal and intrinsic integration," is to establish the reciprocity of constituting act and constituted object. Habits solicit certain reactions to a perceived object; reciprocally, the perceived object solicits certain responses from the field of habitual meanings. The resulting total solicitation represents a "fusion" or "blending" of the organism's contribution to the interaction and that of the perceived object.[73]

What is explained here is equivalent to the phenomenological concept of apperception. As we observe an object, our past experience allows us to add those characteristics usually belonging to such objects but not available immediately to perception. We don't need to examine the mouth of a growling dog in order to form the assumption it has teeth. In walking down the city street, we tacitly assume that the buildings surrounding us are not mere facades (as on a movie set) but buildings with rooms, floors, hallways, and other constituents. We make this assumption despite our inability to perceive these features from our street position. These features are predicted. They are apperceived and added spontaneously in consciousness. On this elementary, pre-reflective level, we see object and habit blending in perception. Habits and sensory abilities coordinate to bring an object before consciousness. They allow conscious inquiry into the nature of the object. We perceive the object as it is given, and we add to it those qualities not visible but assumed.

The unity of which Dewey speaks is constitutive. Object and subject unite in the constitutive act. This interpenetration results in the quality which, it must be stressed, is formed pre-reflectively in situations. Dewey stated: "There is nothing intellectual or cognitive in the existence of such situations, although they are the necessary condition for cognitive operations for inquiry. In themselves, they are precognitive."[74] And this "cognitive experience must originate within that of a non-cognitive sort."[75] In another context, Dewey said that "memories, not necessarily conscious but retentions that have been . . . incorporated in the very structure of the self, feed" the observations of men.[76] If we want to understand how reflection is possible, then we must probe the pre-predicative elements of constitutive acts. "An analysis of the mechanism of predicative judgment," said Schutz, "is warranted only by recourses to the mental processes in which and by which pre-predicative experience has been constituted."[77]

This is just the realm Dewey attempts to probe in analyzing the pre-reflective. However, it has been a much-neglected area of Dewey's thought. As a result, many philosophers have assumed that Dewey totally neglected the topic. For example, Schutz has stated "that the many great performances in the field of logic for which our generation is indebted to Dewey's operationalism and James's pragmatism can find their justification only by recourse to the field of pre-predicative experience."[78] If Dewey's investigations of the pre-reflective were more popularly accepted, perhaps Schutz would not have been so quick to assume Dewey neglected the pre-predicative area. This is not to say that Schutz would have found Dewey's ideas totally compatible with his own phenomenology. I only contend that the ideas of the two men were not so divergent in this area as Schutz may have believed.

TOPICAL (THEMATIC) RELEVANCE: DEFINING THE PROBLEMATIC

We can move now from the unproblematic realm, where motivational relevances predominated, and into areas where routines are broken by the unexpected or where the taken-for-granted is no longer adequate to define the situation at hand. Schutz directs us toward this new realm by saying:

> It may happen that not all motivationally relevant elements foreknown in sufficient degrees of familiarity are adequate, or that the situation proves to be one which cannot be referred by synthesis of recognition to a previous situation typically alike, similar, etc., . . . because it is radically new. In such a case it be-

comes necessary to "know more about" these elements, be it that new knowledge must be acquired, be it that the knowledge at hand must be transformed into higher degrees of familiarity.[79]

In such cases, man becomes involved through a higher level of ego activity. The activity is "founded upon motivational relevancy," but, Schutz insisted, "still differs totally from it."[80] Relevances which were taken for granted previously are now rendered questionable and made topics of our attention. Typicality has been violated, and this violation must become thematic in consciousness to re-establish harmony.

During mundane activities, we experience a unity between expectations and perceptions in what Schutz calls the "field of the unproblematic."[81] When this pre-reflective unity is broken, a "tension" develops between what is expected and what is perceived. This tension is constituted in consciousness and is characterized by a reordering of the thematic field. At least temporarily, previous concerns are released from the mind's grip and replaced by a new thematic kernel. The problem is now "thematically" or "topically" relevant. (Schutz uses the terms interchangeably.) As Schutz explains the process: "To make an object a problem, to make it the theme or topic of our thought, means nothing else than to conceive it as . . . dubious and questionable [and] to segregate it from the background of unquestionable and unquestioned familiarity which is simply taken for granted."[82]

The retrieval of things from the shadowed horizons of the taken-for-granted may be a voluntary act of the ego—an individual moves from the status of "knowledge of acquaintance" to the status of "knowledge about."[83] Or prevailing conditions within the situation can bring things from horizon to focus. For this reason, topical relevances, like relevances of the motivational variety, can be intrinsic (volitional) or imposed.[84] In either case, experience is intrinsically open to further expansion. As long as the horizons of any field of consciousness are accessible to reflection and inquiry, the boundaries of knowledge are nearly infinite. (This insight is essential to understanding Dewey's thoughts on education, but it would be out of place to elaborate this point here.)

Topical relevances contain implications for solving the problem at hand. There is a dual directionality inherent in the workings of motivational and topical relevances. Motivational relevances account for the selectivity of consciousness and the formation of our interest

in a topic. This interest may be circumscribed only vaguely and experienced as a "sense" that something is amiss. This "sense of a
problem," as Dewey used to call it, demands that we halt on-going
activity. As both Dewey and Schutz repeated often, we must "stop
and think." Up to this point, nothing particularly intellectual or cognitive is alive in the situation; it is "precognitive."[85] But when we
stop and think, we turn our reflective attention to the situation and
make it the subject of inquiry. "In every case where reflective activity ensues," Dewey said, "there is a process of *intellectualizing* what
at first is merely an *emotional* quality of the whole situation." (Dewey's italics.)[86]

In reflection on-going action stops, and our attention is turned
back to the sensed interruption. The first step of inquiry involves a
backward glance of consciousness: the situation is reevaluated to
define the problem at hand. Despite focus on the past, this process
carries strong implications for the future. The mere thematization
of the problematic, said Dewey, "represents the partial transformation by inquiry of a problematic situation into a determinate situation. . . . The way in which the problem is conceived decides what
specific suggestions are entertained and which are dismissed; what
data are selected and which are rejected; *it is the criterion for relevancy and irrelevancy of hypotheses and conceptual structures.*"
(Italics added.) In short, Dewey said that the constituted problem
"has, in the very terms of its statement, reference to a possible solution."[87] The solution is a hoped-for future occurrence, but it is connected inherently to the present because it is implied in the
definition of the problem. The pre-reflective sensing of a problem
necessitates a backward glance and implicates the past. The definition of the problem prefigures the future.

The topical relevance structure brings the problem into relief.
Schutz even said that "the thematically relevant is the problem. . . .
It solicits us to penetrate into its inner and outer horizons, to bring
it, in a synthesis of recognition, to coincidence with elements con-
tained in our stock of knowledge. . . ." Note the interconnection of
these relevance structures. The problem is defined by topical relevances, and clarification implies its solution. But it still stands out
against the background of motivational relevances which are on the
horizon of the newly constituted field of consciousness. This makes
it possible for Schutz to say that it is the "motivational relevancies
which determine the conditions under which the problem involved

in the theme could be considered as solved. . . ."[88] We referred earlier to the fact that not everything can become problematic at once. As Schutz said, "The problematic emerges on the foundation of the unproblematic, and the unknown refers to the familiar. . . ."[89] The problem is formed in the structures of topical relevance. But these structures are only the thematic focus within a wider field. Behind them stretches a background of unquestioned motivational relevances, amounting to the "because-motivation" for the problem's existence.

The final solution to the problem, the adjusted state which re-establishes harmony, is not, said Dewey, an "absolute end-in-itself, an absolute good by which to determine what to do. . . ."[90] Rather, the problem is resolved when the conditions alive within the situation are satisfied. Motivational relevances which brought the problem into consciousness therefore are involved in the solution to it. They play a referential role in rendering any solution warranted. They can limit the inquiry by suggesting what is necessary to render an indeterminate situation determinate. As Schutz pointed out, the extent of any investigation is "determined by the level at which we break off further investigation as immaterial and irrelevant for [the] purposes at hand."[91] That decision is made when the conditions of the situation are satisfied. In some situations, this may involve changing our stock of knowledge at hand; in others, manipulating the environment. Both kinds of changes are likely to occur. The differences between these situations, however, are only ones of emphasis.[92] It is clear in either case that motivational relevances are implicated in the outcome of the problematic situation.

INTERPRETATIVE RELEVANCE: DIRECTIONS OF INQUIRY

Once a phenomenon has been given thematically to an individual as problematic and open for interpretation, another set of relevances is presented. The problematic is disquieting; it causes us to seek a resolution. As Peirce wrote in 1877, "Doubt is an uneasy and dissatisfied state from which we struggle to free ourselves and pass into the state of belief. . . ."[93] The problematic object must be inquired into. By virtue of its typicality, Schutz said, it must finally be subsumed "under the various typical prior experiences which constitute [an individual's] stock of knowledge at hand."[94] This may entail some revision within typicality structures, within the environment, or within both. But what is important is that the unknown can be interpreted only on the basis of what is known. However, not everything within our stock of knowledge is relevant to the problem at hand. Man brings into his interpretative scheme only those things he believes to be connected in some way to the problem, only that which is of *"interpretative relevance."*

In discussing interpretative relevance, it may help to alter slightly our shirt-in-the-corner example. Schutz made the example more complex by asking readers to imagine a man entering a room and becoming aware of something coiled in the corner. The man could not distinguish readily what that something was, but he could perceive enough of the object (size, color, shape, etc.) to establish pre-reflectively some eidetic possibilities. It could have been an article of clothing distorted by insufficient light to appear ropelike or snakelike —or it could have been a rope or a snake. The object was not perceived in a vacuum but entered the man's consciousness surrounded by horizons which gave the object definition.[95] The man perceived not an insulated object but an object of specifiable possibilities: it was a shirt, a rope, or a snake.[96] These possibilities occurred in the perceptual processes of passive synthesis, that is, they occurred pre-reflectively.

The man's habits in this example have been taken to their pre-reflective limits. He can go no further without more information, that is, until the situation is altered in some way. At this point, the man can wait for outside forces to change the situation: he might wait for dawn to break and cast more light, or he can take steps and of his own volition alter the situation. Interpretative relevances of the latter variety could be called intrinsic or volitional. Schutz showed that they differ from imposed relevances, because the imposed variety is "directed toward perception (as in the prepredicative sphere)," whereas the volitional acts forming the intrinsic interpretative relevance structures of the problematic situation are "directed toward knowledge." The difference is that "knowledge," as Schutz uses the term, "is a form of spontaneous activity with the purpose not of producing objects . . . but of becoming better and better acquainted with the pregiven object." In Dewey's language, imposed interpretative relevances are directed toward "perception." The ego activity involved in volitional and interpretative relevance is a higher order. It cannot be characterized by the passive receptivity of apperception; rather, it is characterized by the spontaneous activities of conceptual thinking.[97] Material on the horizon must be divested systematically of its taken-for-granted quality and made the topic or theme of investigation.

The man in the room confronts an object which presents equally plausible explanations, none of which present sufficient evidence to allow a warranted conclusion. The man must feed more information into the problem. He may ask himself what he knows about snakes and ropes that is relevant to this situation. He may remember that snakes are apt to move if threatened. Were he to disturb the object in the corner and it responded by moving, the man would be better able to make a warranted judgment of the object's identity. Definitely it would not be a shirt or a rope; probably it would turn out to be a snake. But let us go further with Schutz's example. The man may also lift from his stock of knowledge the fact that snakes don't take kindly to being disturbed, even in the name of scientific inquiry: they are apt to react with hostility. This may be particularly relevant if the man is cowardly and recalls that some snakes are poisonous. He may decide not to touch the snake but to throw a shoe at the coiled object and observe its reactions from a safe distance.

This example implies a great deal. The man is probing the horizons of his knowledge for information relevant to a warranted identification of the object. The horizontal knowledge of snakes which presented the object as unknown, but possibly a snake, was elevated to the thematic. What the man discovered about the snake was insufficient to solve the problem. The object could be identified as a snake if it moved. But until it did so, the situation would remain problematic. Thus, on the basis of knowledge deemed interpretatively relevant, a hypothesis was formed and tested in fantasy. The man concluded that the unidentified something would be a snake, if it moved when he threw a shoe at it. Thus, a hypothesis is formed by exploring the horizons of the problem for interpretatively relevant material. This material is the criterion for judging the consequences of proposed action. As Schutz said (making appropriate reference to Dewey), "Only by considering the act as accomplished can we judge whether the contemplated means of bringing it about are appropriate or not. . . ."[98]

The similarities between Schutz's analysis of how men deal with problematic situations and the analysis offered by Dewey are obvious. "Deliberation," said Dewey, "is an experiment in finding out what the various lines of possible action are really like. It is an experiment in making various combinations of selected elements of habit and impulses, to see what the resultant action would be like if it were entered upon. But the trial is in imagination, not in overt fact."[99] This amounts to a tentative and dramatic rehearsal in imagination. Schutz was very interested in Dewey's thought on this matter and refers more frequently to this portion of Dewey's work than to any other. At least seven references to it can be found in Schutz's writings.

Other hypotheses may be available to the man. Perhaps the object is the shirt he wore the day before. Perhaps his son was using a rope for some Boy Scout activity. Each of these possibilities is forceful enough to render doubtful the others. But neither is forceful enough to settle the matter or, as Dewey put it, "to become the center of a re-directed activity." Habitual activity therefore is transformed into reflective activity. "Activity does not cease in order to give way to reflection," wrote Dewey. "Activity is turned from execution into intra organic channels, resulting in dramatic rehearsal." These rehearsals are the way an individual can deal with his contending preferences—it is an excess, not the absence, of preferences which causes the redirection of on-going action into reflective thought. To quote Dewey again: "Choice is not the emergence of preference out of indifference. It is the emergence of a unified preference out of competing preferences."[100]

In a situation of competing preferences, said Schutz, "postulate stands against postulate, one contests the other and is contested by the other. In . . . a doubtful situation both beliefs . . . have the character of being 'questionable,' and that which is questionable is always contested . . . by something else. The ego oscillates between two [or more] tendencies. . . ."[101] Schutz later amended the term "oscillate," or at least clarified it. "Many authors, including Husserl," he said, "seem inclined to conceive the hesitation between doubtful interpretations as an oscillating between two themes. . . . Contrary to this, we submit that only one theme prevails throughout the whole process as paramount. What is thematic is always the percept of this same strange object in the corner of my room. . . . At least we may say, the noema of this percept remains unchanged despite all possible noetical variations." Schutz meant that the intentional object is apperceived as problematic, as an object of a determinable indeterminance. It is not first a shirt and then a rope and then a snake, but until determination is warranted, it is a shirt or a rope or a snake object. The *noema* of the percept is a problem-object, and it is this problem-object which "remains my homebase, my paramount theme which is never out of [my] grip" for as long as the problem lasts.[102]

Schutz's clarification may move him away from Husserl on this point, but simultaneously it moves him closer to Dewey. No significance for this fact is claimed beyond the boundaries of this narrow topic. Nevertheless, one should note Schutz's insistence that it is the problem of contending possibilities which is thematic in consciousness, rather than the possibilities themselves. The possibilities arise in context by virtue of a problem which pervades the entire situation with a specific quality. We do not oscillate between isolated possible definitions of the object in question, "for we never experience nor form judgments about objects and events in isolation, but only in connection with a contextual whole. This latter is what is called a 'situation,'" said Dewey.[103] Such quotes from Dewey usually and correctly are taken to mean that objects appear in a field which is funded by subjective and objective conditions within environment. This has been argued earlier in the study. The point can be expanded slightly by suggesting that competing preferences must also be regarded as belonging within a unitary situation and should not be seen as isolated, singular objects. Schutz seems to make this point in criticizing Husserl's notion of oscillation. It is the problem-object which is thematic in the consciousness of the man. That sensed problem accounts for the quality of the entire situation and funds each of the contending preferences with meaning.

7. The Recovery of Experience in Sociology

The visible is set in the invisible; and in the end what is unseen decides what happens in the seen; the tangible rests precariously on the untouched and ungrasped.

John Dewey, *Experience and Nature*

No DISCIPLINE can wall itself off totally from the influence of the culture in which it operates. No scientist can ignore the fact that he is a man among other men. In a sense, then, there may be no such thing as *purely* objective science. "All knowledge of cultural reality, as may be seen," Max Weber claimed, "is always knowledge from *particular points of view*." (Weber's italics.)[1] Advances made by science cannot be credited to unsullied objectivity, but to man's systematic and doggedly determined efforts to approach a totally objective stance. This implies that science would not have advanced if its connections with culture were simply ignored. Science proceeds productively only as it makes these connections explicit.

Schutz reminds us that science is a human activity, and that the "basis of meaning . . . in every science is the pre-scientific life-world. . . ."[2] Thus, the links between science and the life-world cannot be broken. In the human pursuit of science, the most we can accomplish is to hold in abeyance the influences of everyday life. This operation preserves man's connections with his life-world yet brackets them for scientific purposes. It demands that these connections be examined and explained. Only through conscious effort can a scientist approach a solitary stance and find a degree of detachment from his social environment and social relationships. Only by clarifying his values can he bracket them and take up the work of value-free science.

This need for explicitness exists in all scientific disciplines, but perhaps nowhere more urgently than in the social sciences. Current

efforts to expunge objectivity from the social sciences and to give
free rein to the individual values of the practitioners threaten not
only the validity of results, but more important, the validity of social
science as science. Such efforts certainly run contrary to the hopes
Dewey and Schutz had for the scientific study of man and culture.

The present tendency to let values loose in the social sciences is
disturbing, but perhaps no more so than a longtime tendency to
smuggle them into social theory beneath the camouflage of self-
acclaimed objectivity. When this is done, sociologists offer only
"naive, pseudo-solutions" to the pressing problems confronting their
discipline. These solutions, Schutz has commented, are "generated
from subjective biases which may be temperamental, political or at
best metaphysical." Schutz points out that a priori solutions run
counter to the most cherished "principle of scientific research, the
principle which calls upon us simply to understand and describe the
facts before us." When values or the commonsense assumptions of
our everyday lives "are uncritically admitted into the apparatus of a
science," warns Schutz, "they have a way of taking their revenge."[3]
That revenge usually takes the form of erroneous sociological theory
and misinterpretation of social facts. Perhaps unwittingly, the social
scientist serves not science but some unnamed and unexamined bias
which exists below the level of his reflective gaze.

While many of the criticisms of, and plans for, sociology presented
by Alvin Gouldner in *The Coming Crisis of Western Sociology* are
disturbing, he makes a worthwhile request that sociologists examine
their own professional behavior as meticulously as they examine the
behavior of others. Dubbing this adventure in professional self-
examination "Reflexive Sociology," Gouldner demands that "we
sociologists must—at the very least—acquire the ingrained *habit* of
viewing our own beliefs as we now view those held by others." This
requires, he insists, "that sociologists must surrender the assumption,
as wrongheaded as it is human, that others believe out of need while
we believe—only or primarily—because of the dictates of logic and
evidence."[4]

Gouldner chose to view reflexive sociology as a moral undertaking.
In the present age, perhaps it is more comfortable to work in the
name of morality than in the name of science. Yet on the face of it,
one can hardly deny that Gouldner is calling on sociology to become
more self-consciously scientific. In that cause he should be supported.

Sociology as a discipline was born in the tumult following the French Revolution. This point is significant to the course sociological theory has taken. The intellectual and political upheavals of the time had cast doubt on the taken-for-granted assumptions of that society. It became possible for individuals to question what had hitherto been unquestionable. Society had been cut open, and its innards were exposed for inspection by philosophers and others of speculative dispositions. What is significant, however, is a current in sociology that from the very beginning wore down the banks of science and moved toward a lowland Utopia of psychological security and certitude.

Auguste Comte, for example, envisioned an absolutely perfect world, an organic society discovered, organized, and ruled by sociology. The disorganized state of his society would be brought under the control of a dogmatic science, and men would unite at last in the mutual worship of unification. There were laws of nature, Comte contended, that when violated by human caprice rained terror in the hearts and minds of men. Comte's quest to discover these laws was nothing less than an attempt to salvage his sanity and regain the "liberty" that accompanies order, predictability, and harmony. "True liberty," he informed his readers, "is nothing else than a rational submission to the preponderance of laws of nature, in release from all arbitrary personal dictation."[5] If Comte's view of science was dogmatic, we must at least grant him the point that in a world where nothing can be taken for granted, all human acts are in fact arbitrary. No wonder, then, that Comte sought to escape chaos and hoped to discover "the fundamental sequence of the various events of human history," which he was sure could be explained "according to a single design."[6]

What Comte did in postrevolutionary France has been repeated since by myriad sociologists. He put sociology in service of a Utopian vision. Science is endangered, however, when its findings are verified by some arbitrary measure or vision. If we fail to take social facts as they are found and instead select only those facts which will serve some Utopian vision, then we are not scientists but idealogues. Science crumbles under the weight of superimposed, a priori solutions to problems.

Comte is used only to illustrate a kind of problem still rampant in sociological theory: the problem of a priori solutions smuggled into scientific inquiry by the taken-for-granted assumptions of social scientists. Sociology is unlikely to liberate its practitioners from either the agonies of chaos or the oppressive nature of totalitarian order, if we let the aim of "liberation" displace that of unbiased understanding.

If sociology offers any form of liberation at all, it would be only the liberation accompanying deeper knowledge and a fuller understanding of human affairs. But it guarantees no outcomes and promises no conclusions about the state of the human condition. It offers neither an outline of a fixed, Utopian future nor a guaranteed procedure for obtaining desired ends.

The liberating features of sociology rest in the disciplined attempt to reach beyond the taken-for-granted assumptions of any social order and to scrutinize scientifically all human institutions. Sociology thus is made possible not by an attitude which demands order, but by the sociologist's willingness to be astonished. This willingness to endure ambiguity, to open the self to whatever lies behind standard interpretations offered by society, to question prevailing definitions of reality, including one's own, is the only liberating mechanism sociology is likely to provide. Sociology may give its practitioners good reason to respect order. But the everyday workings of the sociologist must be in a sense subversive. Sociology is a debunking discipline, as Peter Berger has labeled it.[7] The most it dares promise those who respect its scientific integrity is a new humility born in discovery of the precarious nature of social reality.[8]

The tumultuous decade of the 1960s brought into American sociology many young radicals whose hopes for the discipline are as misplaced as those of Comte. As Berger has pointed out, many of these people see "sociology [as] nothing less than the theoretical arm of revolutionary praxis, that is, a liberating discipline in the literal sense of a radical transformation of the social order."[9] Insofar as this quest for liberation is satisfied by a fuller understanding of the workings of society, would-be revolutionaries are likely to find satisfaction in the confines of sociology. However, if they wish to substitute the revolutionary temperament for the relevance structures of science, their work is unlikely to amount to anything more than historical curiosity. This does not mean that sociological findings may not be of use to many people, revolutionaries included. It only states that sociological work necessarily must serve science and not some ideological end.

We have been using extreme examples in order to make the point that sociological theory has frequently been guided by the ulterior motives of the sociological theorist. As we have tried to indicate, the danger is present in a more subtle manner than our examples might suggest. If we looked carefully, we would find it in many elaborate and seemingly scientific theories which offer monolithic explanations for all forms of human behavior. Even a cursory view of current theories would reveal such unidimensional explanations for human events as man's acquisitive nature, his aggressive instincts or will to power, his sexual drives, or his social nature and his territorial imperatives. Our argument here is not against the usefulness of these models; it is directed at the Procrustean tendencies of some of their devotees to hold them up as the only valid measures of human behavior. For example, rather than say that human beings sometimes behave in an economic mode, some claim that the model of exchange exhausts human possibilities and that an overwhelming desire to maximize gain propels every experience. No doubt the exchange model has something to offer science, but it certainly does more damage than good when it solidifies into what is offered as natural law.

To claim that men behave only to maximize gain and minimize loss, and that they do so because of some immutable, inborn propulsion, hides vast portions of human behavior from view. To inquire into the social origins of value, for example, becomes superfluous. It becomes difficult to investigate the constitution of meaning or to probe the workings of consciousness; men, it would seem, are conscious only of avenues available to profit and loss.

When single-cause explanations are attributed to all human events, man as a conscious being is lost in the resulting explanations of his behavior. He is made the hapless puppet of a single, externally imposed force. (To make the claim that this force is instinctive does not, of course, make it any less external.) The nature of these single forces varies greatly from one school of social behavior to another. But all such schools seem united in unstated determination to eliminate consciousness as a significant factor in human behavior.

They are united in a second and related area. Unitary explanations of human behavior usually transform what is observed into causal explanations for man's actions. For example, if man is found to be aggressive, this behavior is attributed to his aggressive nature. If he is found to run in groups, this fact is attributed to his social nature. In this regard, some social scientists have not progressed significantly beyond the Greek argument that apples fall because they are endowed naturally with an attribute of "fallingness."

Dewey terms such conclusions "lazy fallacies." He points out that we must not appeal to a gregarious instinct to explain social arrangements: such a procedure mistakes the event for its cause. It replicates "in a so-called causal force the effects to be accounted for." Dewey claimed that such arguments are of a piece with the claim that opium puts man to sleep "because of its dormative powers." He said: "Men do not run together and join in a larger mass as do drops of quicksilver, and if they did the result would not be a state nor any mode of human association. The instincts, whether named gregariousness, or sympathy, or the sense of mutual dependence . . . at best account for everything in general and nothing in particular. And at worst, the alleged instinct and natural endowment appealed to as a causal force themselves represent psychological tendencies which have previously been shaped into habits of action and expectation by means of the very social conditions they are supposed to explain."[10]

Sociology has a primary task to investigate the ways in which the social tendencies Dewey referred to are shaped into "habits of action and expectation." Further, it is essential that the role of habit in experience be explained and that sociology take into account the genesis and organization of human experience. In short, sociology must confront the workings of human consciousness. By doing so, sociologists will be able to check the tendency to regard social theory as a monolithic, natural law. They will have to reject theories which have neither reference nor relationship to the world of everyday life. Rather than allowing themselves the ill-conceived assumption that everything transpires between men at the hand of some omnipotent causal force, sociologists will have to return to the actual events of human experience to understand human behavior. They will have to account for human consciousness and greet it on its own terms, checking their developing theories not against theoretical first principles, but against everyday activities.

This has been the central theme of Alfred Schutz's work. It bears a striking resemblance to Dewey's insistence that twentieth-century philosophy can no longer ignore everyday events in the wrong-headed assumption that reality lies elsewhere. Philosophy, Dewey insisted, must deal with reality where it is found, in the events of everyday life. It must take "its stand with daily life, which finds that . . . things really have to be reckoned with as they occur interwoven in the texture of events." If philosophy remains convinced that it must work on another plane in search of "a Reality . . . superior to the events of everyday occurrence," the result will be an "increasing isolation of philosophy from common sense and science."[11] Just as Dewey identifies "the need for a recovery of philosophy," so does Schutz call for the recovery of sociology.

This call need not expel from the discipline any sociologist or any particular theory. It merely insists that sociologists hold theory accountable to human experience. As long as that is done, a plurality of hypotheses would be welcome within sociological theory. As Dewey pointed out long ago, "[A] plurality of alternatives is the effective means of rendering inquiry more extensive, . . . more flexible, more capable of taking cognizance of all the facts that are discovered."[12]

The most significant consequence of the single-cause approach to social science is the propensity to ignore human intelligence. Social science must start from man's actions and not from preconceived causes for such actions. We cannot ignore the meanings which actors ascribe to their actions. These meanings must be confronted on their own terms rather than forced into preformed conceptions of what all actions mean to the social scientist. In order to do this, the social scientist must be totally aware of his own presuppositions. His conceptions must not be taken for granted. Dewey was correct when he said that "failure to examine the conceptual structures and frames of reference which are unconsciously implicated in even the seemingly most innocent factual inquiries is the greatest single defect that can be found in any field of inquiry."[13]

Schutz contends that the social sciences must come to terms with the experiences of men as they are lived by the actors themselves. He calls on sociologists to "go back to the 'forgotten man' of the social sciences, to the actor in the social world whose doing and feeling lies at the bottom of the whole system." Schutz says that we must "try to understand [man] in that doing and feeling and the state of mind which induced him to adopt specific attitudes towards his environment." Sociology can be content no longer with explaining the social world in terms of its meanings to the social scientist. No longer can it subjugate itself to the social scientist's lust for certitude. It must ask, What does this social world mean to subject "A" as he acts within it? What do his actions mean to him? What are the in-order-to-motives which propel him and what because-motives compel his actions? When we ask these questions, "we no longer naively accept the social world and its current idealizations and formalizations as ready-made and meaningful beyond all question, but we undertake to study the process of idealizing and formalizing as such, the genesis of meaning [and] the mechanism of the activity by which human beings understand one another and themselves."[14] These questions cannot be avoided by anyone who takes sociology seriously.

As Schutz has put it, "Only after we have a firm grasp of the concept of meaning as such will we be able to analyze step by step the meaning-structure of the social world."[15] To accomplish this, sociology must confront the philosophical question of human experience and must investigate problems of relevance.

"All experiences and all acts are grounded on relevance structures," said Schutz and Luckmann. "Every decision more or less explicitly introduces, besides the actor, a series of relevances. The relevance problem is perhaps the most important and at the same time the most difficult problem that the description of the life-world has to solve."[16] Sociology cannot ignore human consciousness and its powers of intentionality, motive, and meaning. The recording and intricate mathematical tabulation of human action are insufficient to totally explain human behavior. External indications are not enough. Sociology must look beyond them "into the constituting process within the living consciousness" of the subjects under study.[17] As Natanson has said, sociology must develop "a way of looking at social phenomena which takes into primary account the intentional structure of human consciousness, and which accordingly places major emphasis on the meaning social acts have for the actors who perform them and who live in a reality built out of their subjective interpretations."[18]

The wisdom of reestablishing experience as the foundation of sociological theory is indisputable. But we should not ignore the objective power of cultural reality, nor should we retreat into introspective psychology. Quite the opposite is the case. Experience has an integral and dialectic connection with both ego and world, the subjective and the objective. Contrary to the claims of some "privatists," individual consciousness is not the only thing of significance in the world. There are realities over which consciousness has little or no control. As Egon Bittner, a sociologist of the phenomenological persuasion, has put it:

Despite the fact that I have (together with the rest of mankind, of course) an enormous span of control over the world surrounding me . . . it remains a melancholy truth that the world as a whole will always have its way with me, in the long run. . . . Wisdom in the exercise of freedom—or simply reasonableness—consists of aligning one's will with the immutable urgencies that inhere in the realities of circumstance. What else is folly if not the neglect of or oblivion to the intractabilities of the world?[19]

The question is not trivial, especially coming from a phenomenologist. When phenomenology runs amuck, its errors generally are on the side of glorifying subjectivity to the neglect of any reality other than that found in the solitary ego. This position not only distorts sociology beyond all recognition (indeed, making all social sciences impossible), but—if my experience with its proponents is at all representative—seriously challenges the possibility of civil intercourse. That view not only denies realism, but as Bittner says, "it . . . become[s], in effect, a factor in the estrangement between man and world [and] also signals a retreat from unity among men."[20] It is unlikely that abortive phenomenology can salvage sociology from its present dilemmas. It can serve only as a somewhat pretentious intellectual product of the increased tendencies toward privatization in the modern world.[21]

The recovery of experience in the social sciences may remind functionalists of the existence of human consciousness. But it should be no less a reminder to crypto-idealists that there is more to the world than individual sensitivities. The question for sociology is not whether to side with man or culture, individual or institution. The task is to confront and understand both man and world in their unification through experience.

This study has not focused on questions of methodology. We have not concerned ourselves with the vast and intricate problems regarding accessibility to outside observation of the subjective elements of experience. We refer the reader to the elaborate, although by no means complete, answers Schutz found to these questions. Our purpose has been to join Dewey and Schutz in a philosophical exploration of the genesis and organization of experience in order to better define the sociological task. Only on this level can a theoretical foundation for sociology be established.

In clarifying the organization and structure of human experience, we uncovered many areas in which the philosophies of Dewey and Schutz complement each other to a great degree, at least in the problem areas of relevance and experience. We have demonstrated that:

1. Because of their philosophic attitudes, Dewey and Schutz attempted to understand more fully man's relationship with his world.
2. Many of Schutz's criticisms of pragmatism are unwarranted if applied to Dewey.
3. Dewey's use of the term "environment" and Schutz's idea of the "life-world" complement each other to a great degree.
4. The phenomenological explanation of consciousness as a field is consistent with Dewey's explanation of consciousness.
5. The idea of typification coincides with a portion of what Dewey subsumes under his notion of habit.
6. Pragmatism's insistence on the unification of subject and object in experience exists also in Schutz's phenomenology, and the idea of relevance makes little sense unless it is explained in this naturalistic mode.
7. Relevance in its various forms parallels Dewey's "stages" of experience as follows:
    a) Motivational relevance is comparable to Dewey's ideas on the pre-reflective and qualitative elements of experience.
    b) Topical or thematic relevance parallels what Dewey referred to as "problem formation."
    c) Interpretative relevance parallels Dewey's explanation of inquiry and reflective thought.

It must be acknowledged that this analysis has proceeded without reference to the social and cultural influences on experience. A clearer explanation of experience was thought possible if these elements were eliminated. Their absence should not suggest privatization of human experience. We must acknowledge, as Schutz does, that "the world as taken for granted is not my private world, nor, for the most part, are the systems of relevance. Knowledge is from the outset socialized knowledge, and thus, too, are the systems of relevances and the world taken for granted."[22] This point can be emphasized further by remembering how concerned Dewey was with questions of social and cultural influence on human behavior.

The various forms of relevance and various stages of experience discussed in this study were separated for clarity's sake and are not divisible in reality. Schutz contended that "the three systems of relevances are . . . but three aspects of a single set of phenomena." The "interrelationship among the types of relevances should not be taken as chronological. . . . All three types are concretely experienced as inseparable or, at least as an individual unity, and their dissection from experience into three types is the result of an analysis of their constitutive origin."[23] Schutz is again very close to Dewey, and this observation can serve as our final indication that the ideas of the two men were complementary. Dewey insisted that his phases of experience "do not follow one another in set order. On the contrary, each step in genuine thinking does something to perfect the formation of a suggestion and promote its change into a leading idea or directive hypothesis . . . . We point out that the . . . phases of reflection that have been described represent only in outline the indispensable traits of reflective thinking. In practice, two of them may telescope, some of them may be passed over hurriedly. . . . No set rules can be set down in such matters."[24]

Despite the differences between the thoughts of Dewey and Schutz, we hope this study has captured something of the respect these men had for the wonders of human consciousness. From their common interest in the motility of consciousness spring all other similarities in their thoughts. If their conclusions are sometimes at variance with one another, those differences may be of little moment. As Dewey put it in a letter to a colleague who found himself at odds with some of Dewey's ideas:

> As philosophers, our disagreements with one another as to conclusions are trivial in comparison with our disagreements as to problems; to see the problem another sees, in the same perspective and at the same angle—that amounts to something. Agreement as to conclusions is in comparison perfunctory.[25]

Notes

Chapter 1

1. John Dewey, *The Quest for Certainty* (New York: G. P. Putnam's Sons, Capricorn Books, 1960), p. 6.
2. Ibid., p. 10.
3. Thomas Luckmann has pointed out that the division of man and cosmos began to emerge with the formalization of religion in primitive societies. For this to happen, "the technology of production and the division of labor must be sufficiently developed to permit the accumulation of surplus over the subsistence minimum." *The Invisible Religion* (New York: Macmillan Co., 1970), pp. 63–64. Further evidence is found in the disturbing yet important book by Colin Turnbull, *The Mountain People* (New York: Simon & Schuster, 1972), pp. 183–208.
4. Dewey, *Quest for Certainty*, pp. 16–17.
5. Ibid., p. 228.
6. John Dewey, *Experience and Nature*, 2d ed. (New York: Dover Publications, 1958), pp. 158, 68.
7. Ibid., p. 69.
8. See Dewey, *Quest for Certainty*; and idem, *Philosophy and Civilization* (Gloucester, Mass.: Peter Smith, 1968).
9. Isaiah Berlin, *The Age of Enlightenment: The Eighteenth Century Philosophers*, Great Ages of Western Philosophy Series, 6 vols. (Freeport, N.Y.: Books for Libraries Press, 1970), 4:18.
10. Ibid., pp. 27–28.
11. Quoted in Albert Salomon, *The Tyranny of Progress: Reflections on the Origins of Sociology* (New York: Noonday Press, 1955), p. 100.
12. John B. Watson, *Behaviorism* (Chicago: University of Chicago Press, Phoenix Books, 1958), p. 6.
13. Ibid., p. 44.
14. Ibid., pp. 104, 304.
15. Robert Woodworth, *Contemporary Schools of Psychology* (New York: Ronald Press, 1948), p. 94.
16. Watson, *Behaviorism*, p. 250.
17. Woodworth, *Contemporary Schools of Psychology*, p. 215.
18. Max Scheler, *Man's Place in Nature*, trans. Hans Meyerhoff (New York: Farrar, Straus & Cudahy, Noonday Press, 1969), pp. 51–55.
19. Quoted in Floyd W. Matson, *The Broken Image: Man, Science, and Society* (Garden City, N.Y.: Doubleday & Co., 1966), p. 30.
20. For a discussion of this topic, see Peter L. Berger, *Invitation to Sociology: A Humanistic Perspective* (Garden City, N.Y.: Doubleday & Co., Anchor Books, 1963), pp. 122–25.

21. Quoted in Matson, *Broken Image*, p. 147.

22. Ernest Becker, *Beyond Alienation* (New York: George Braziller, 1967), p. 126.

23. John Dewey et al., *Creative Intelligence: Essays in the Pragmatic Attitude* (New York: Henry Holt & Co., 1917), pp. 63–64.

24. This point has been thoughtfully and humorously made by Fritz Machlup, who asked how the natural sciences would be affected if scientists were one day to discover that matter could talk. "If Matter Could Talk," in Sidney Morgenbesser, Patrick Suppes, and Morton White, eds., *Philosophy, Science, and Method: Essays in Honor of Ernest Nagel* (New York: St. Martin's Press, 1969), pp. 286–305.

25. John Dewey, "The Need for a Recovery of Philosophy," in Richard J. Bernstein, ed., *On Experience, Nature and Freedom* (Indianapolis, Ind.: Bobbs-Merrill Co., Liberal Arts Press, 1960), p. 69.

26. Richard J. Bernstein, *John Dewey*, Great American Thinker Series (New York: Washington Square Press, 1966), p. 178.

Chapter 2

1. Helmut R. Wagner, ed., *Alfred Schutz on Phenomenology and Social Relations: Selected Writings* (Chicago: University of Chicago Press, 1970), p. 2.

2. Alfred Schutz, *The Phenomenology of the Social World*, trans. George Walsh and Frederic Lehnert (Evanston, Ill.: Northwestern University Press, 1967), p. xxxii.

3. Maurice Natanson, "Alfred Schutz on Social Reality and Social Science," *Social Research* 35 (1968):242.

4. José Ortega y Gasset, *Man and People* (New York: W. W. Norton & Co., 1963); Raymond Aron, *Introduction to the Philosophy of History* (Boston: Beacon Press, 1961); Felix Kaufmann, *Methodology of the Social Sciences* (New York: Oxford University Press, 1944); and Ludwig von Mises, *Human Action* (London: William Hodge, 1949).

5. Schutz, *Phenomenology of the Social World*, p. xviii.

6. Alfred Schutz and Thomas Luckmann, *The Structures of the Life-World* (Evanston, Ill.: Northwestern University Press, 1973), p. xix.

7. Natanson, "Alfred Schutz on Social Reality," pp. 242, 243.

8. Bruce Wilshire, *William James and Phenomenology: A Study of the "Principles of Psychology"* (Bloomington: Indiana University Press, 1968), p. 4.

9. Alfred Schutz, "Some Leading Concepts of Phenomenology," in idem, *Collected Papers Vol. 1: The Problem of Social Reality*, ed. Maurice Natanson, 3d ed. (The Hague: Martinus Nijhoff, 1962), p. 99.

10. Lester E. Embree, ed., *Life-World and Consciousness: Essays for Aron Gurwitsch* (Evanston, Ill.: Northwestern University Press, 1972), p. xxvi.

11. Maurice Natanson, "The Phenomenology of Alfred Schutz," *Inquiry* 9 (1966):155.

12. Alfred Schutz, "The Stranger: An Essay in Social Psychology," in idem, *Collected Papers Vol. 2: Studies in Social Theory*, ed. Arvid Broderson (The Hague: Martinus Nijhoff, 1964), p. 99.

13. Embree, *Life-World and Consciousness*, p. xxiii.

14. Maurice Natanson, *Phenomenology and Social Reality: Essays in Memory of Alfred Schutz* (The Hague: Martinus Nijhoff, 1970), p. x.

15. See Schutz, *Collected Papers Vol. 1*, p. vi.

16. Alfred Schutz, "The Social World and the Theory of Social Action," *Social Research* 27 (1960):203–21; reprinted in idem, *Collected Papers Vol. 2*, pp. 3–19.

17. Dorion Cairns joined the graduate faculty of the New School for Social Research in 1956, and Schutz worked for many years to bring Gurwitsch to the Department of Philosophy. This was accomplished only after Schutz's sudden death, when Gurwitsch was called to succeed his close friend as professor of philosophy. In 1969, on the tenth anniversary of Schutz's death, the Husserl Archives were established and dedicated to Schutz at the New School.

18. Natanson to author, 25 September 1972.

19. Alfred Schutz, *Reflections on the Problem of Relevance*, ed. Richard M. Zaner (New Haven, Conn.: Yale University Press, 1970), p. xxii.

20. Ilse Schutz to author, 9 November 1972.

21. For a recent discussion of this point, see James L. Heap and Phillip A. Roth, "On Phenomenological Sociology," *American Sociological Review* 38 (June 1973):354–67.

22. Schutz, "On Multiple Realities," in idem, *Collected Papers Vol. 1*, pp. 227–28.

23. See Schutz, *Collected Papers Vol. 1*, p. xxv.

24. Schutz, *Phenomenology of the Social World*, p. 249.

25. See Schutz, *Reflections on the Problems of Relevance*, p. ix.

26. Ibid., pp. xxii–xxiii.

27. Ibid.

28. The unpublished works of Schutz include "Goethes Wilhelm Meisters Lehrjahre" (27 pages) and "Wilhelm Meisters Wanderjahre" (142 pages); "Sinnstruktur der Novelle" (Goethe, about 50 pages); "Entwurf für eine Soziologie der Musik" (a sketch); "Sinnstruktur der Sprache" (a sketch); "Talcott Parson's Theory of Social Action" (74 pages, with a 50-page correspondence with Parsons from 2 February to 17 March 1941); correspondence spanning many years with Eric Voegelin; and an essay on T. S. Eliot's concept of culture. For a complete bibliography of work of and about Schutz, see Natanson, *Phenomenology and Social Reality*, pp. 297–306.

29. Robert J. Roth, *John Dewey and Self-Realization* (Englewood Cliffs, N.J.: Prentice-Hall, 1962), p. 144.

30. Schutz, *Phenomenology of the Social World*, p. 250.

31. John Dewey, "The Theory of Emotion," in Joseph Ratner, ed., *John Dewey: Philosophy, Psychology, and Social Practice* (New York: G. P. Putnam's Sons, Capricorn Books, 1965), p. 242.

32. Maurice Natanson, "Being-in-Reality," *Philosophy and Phenomenological Research* 20 (1959):231–37; reprinted in idem, *Literature, Philosophy, and the Social Sciences: Essays in Existentialism and Phenomenology* (The Hague: Martinus Nijhoff, 1968), pp. 56–61.

33. Natanson, "Being-in-Reality," in *Literature, Philosophy, and the Social Sciences*, pp. 59–60.

34. John Dewey, "Context and Thought," in Richard J. Bernstein, ed., *On Experience, Nature and Freedom* (Indianapolis, Ind.: Bobbs-Merrill Co., Liberal Arts Press, 1960), pp. 92, 98.

35. Natanson, "Being-in-Reality," in *Literature, Philosophy, and the Social Sciences*, p. 60.

36. John Dewey, *Essays in Experimental Logic* (Chicago: University of Chicago Press, 1916), pp. 5–6, 4.

37. Natanson, "Being-in-Reality," in *Literature, Philosophy, and the Social Sciences*, pp. 61, 58.

38. John Dewey, "The Objectivism-Subjectivism of Modern Philosophy," *Journal of Philosophy* 38 (1941):538.

39. Natanson, "Being-in-Reality," in *Literature, Philosophy, and the Social Sciences*, p. 57.

40. John Dewey, *Experience and Nature*, 2d ed. (New York: Dover Publications, 1958), pp. 295, 282.

41. Calvin O. Schrag, *Experience and Being* (Evanston, Ill.: Northwestern University Press, 1969), p. 82.

42. John Dewey, " 'Consciousness' and Experience," in idem, *The Influence of Darwin on Philosophy: And Other Essays in Contemporary Thought* (New York: Peter Smith, 1951), p. 247.

43. Dewey, *Experience and Nature*, p. 411.

44. Jules Altman, Sidney Ratner, and James E. Wheeler, eds., *John Dewey and Arthur F. Bentley: A Philosophical Correspondence, 1932–1951* (New Brunswick, N.J.: Rutgers University Press, 1964), p. 657.

45. W. I. Thomas, *The Child in America* (New York: Alfred A. Knopf, 1928), p. 584.

46. Schutz, *Reflections on Relevance*, p. xxii.

47. A few works have begun to appear on this topic. For example, see Marvin Farber, *Naturalism and Subjectivism* (Albany: State University of New York Press, 1968); Anthony V. Corello, "Some Structural Parallels in Phenomenology and Pragmatism," in Embree, *Life-World and Consciousness*; Victor Kestenbaum, "An Interpretation of Dewey's Notion of Habit from the Perspective of Merleau-Ponty's Phenomenology of the Habitual Body" (Ed.D. diss., Rutgers University, 1972), hereafter referred to as "Dewey's Notion of Habit"; D. C. Mathur, *Naturalistic Philosophies of Experience* (St. Louis, Mo.: Warren H. Green, 1971); Maurice Natanson, *The Social Dynamics of George H. Mead* (Washington, D.C.: Public Affairs Press, 1956); Bruce Wilshire, *William James and Phenomenology*; and John Wild, *The Radical Empiricism of William James* (Garden City, N.Y.: Doubleday & Co., 1969).

48. Natanson to author, 25 September 1972.

49. Ibid.

Chapter 3

1. Alfred Schutz and Thomas Luckmann, *The Structures of the Life-World* (Evanston, Ill.: Northwestern University Press, 1973), pp. 3–4.

2. Alfred Schutz, "On Multiple Realities," in *Collected Papers Vol. 1: The Problem of Social Reality*, ed. Maurice Natanson, 3d ed. (The Hague: Martinus Nijhoff, 1962), p. 229.

3. Schutz and Luckmann, *Structures of the Life-World*, p. 27.

4. Quoted in ibid., p. 30.

5. William James, *The Principles of Psychology*, 2 vols. (New York: Dover Publications, 1950), 2:289.

6. Alfred Schutz, *Reflections on the Problem of Relevance*, ed. Richard M. Zaner (New Haven, Conn.: Yale University Press, 1970), p. 170.

7. John Dewey, *Experience and Nature*, 2d ed. (New York: Dover Publications, 1958), p. 14.

8. John Dewey, *Democracy and Education* (New York: Macmillan Co., Free Press, 1966), pp. 18, 295.

9. Ibid., pp. 295, 18.

10. Dewey, *Experience and Nature*, p. 409.

11. Ibid., pp. 37, 23, 12.

12. Maurice Merleau-Ponty, *Phenomenology of Perception*, trans. Colin Smith (New York: Humanities Press, 1962), p. 120.

13. Herbert Spiegelberg, *The Phenomenological Movement: A Historical Introduction*, 2 vols., 2d ed. (The Hague: Martinus Nijhoff, 1971), 2:534.

14. Bruce Wilshire, *William James and Phenomenology: A Study of the "Principles of Psychology"* (Bloomington: Indiana University Press, 1968), pp. 199–200.

15. John Dewey, "Conduct and Experience in Psychology," in idem, *Philosophy and Civilization* (Gloucester, Mass.: Peter Smith, 1968), p. 264.

16. John Dewey, *Art as Experience* (New York: G. P. Putnam's Sons, Capricorn Books, 1958), p. 247.

17. Edmund Husserl, *Cartesian Meditations: An Introduction to Phenomenology*, trans. Dorion Cairns (The Hague: Martinus Nijhoff, 1960), p. 157.

18. Dewey, *Experience and Nature*, p. 24.

19. Schutz, "Husserl's Importance for the Social Sciences," in idem, *Collected Papers Vol. 1*, p. 149.

20. Peter L. Berger, *Invitation to Sociology: A Humanistic Perspective* (Garden City, N.Y.: Doubleday & Co., Anchor Books, 1963), p. 175. See also idem, "Sociology and Freedom," *American Sociologist* 6 (February 1971):1–5; reprinted in Brigitte Berger, ed., *Readings in Sociology: A Biographical Approach* (New York: Basic Books, 1974), pp. 495–503.

21. Dewey, *Experience and Nature*, pp. 22–23.

22. To deal with a potential argument, Schutz did use the term "transcendence" in referring to the leaving of "finite provinces of meaning of the world of everyday life" and entering other provinces of meaning of reality. Schutz uses that term here, however, not as a goal toward which he directs his work but as the subject of his study. To understand human existence, it is necessary not only to understand that man works at multiple levels of reality and to investigate the structure of these realities, but also to examine the process through which man transcends one level and achieves another.

Chapter 4

1. For Dewey's view on the related issue of mind-body relationships, see "Body and Mind," in idem, *Philosophy and Civilization* (Gloucester, Mass.: Peter Smith, 1968), pp. 299–317.

2. William James, *Essays in Radical Empiricism* (New York: Longmans, Green & Co., 1912), p. 170n.

3. Alfred Schutz, "On Multiple Realities," in idem, *Collected Papers Vol. 1: The Problem of Social Reality*, ed. Maurice Natanson, 3d ed. (The Hague: Martinus Nijhoff, 1962), p. 227.

4. John Dewey, *Experience and Nature*, 2d ed. (New York: Dover Publications, 1958), p. 41.

5. William James, *The Principles of Psychology*, 2 vols. (New York: Dover Publications, 1950), 2:293.

6. Ibid., p. 294.

7. Dewey, *Experience and Nature*, p. 321.

8. Schutz, "On Multiple Realities," in idem, *Collected Papers Vol. 1*, pp. 208–9.

9. Peter L. Berger and Thomas Luckmann, *The Social Construction of Reality: A Treatise in the Sociology of Knowledge* (Garden City, N.Y.: Doubleday & Co., Anchor Books, 1967), p. 22.

10. Peter L. Berger, *The Sacred Canopy* (Garden City, N.Y.: Doubleday & Co., Anchor Books, 1967), p. 20.

11. Alfred Schutz, *Reflections on the Problem of Relevance*, ed. Richard M. Zaner (New Haven, Conn.: Yale University Press, 1970), p. 125.

12. John Dewey, *Democracy and Education* (New York: Macmillan Co., Free Press, 1966), p. 11. I am indebted to Victor Kestenbaum of Boston Uni-

versity for calling my attention to Dewey's use of the term "environment." Dr. Kestenbaum's insights have been of great help to me in this section.

13. John Dewey, *Logic: The Theory of Inquiry* (New York: Henry Holt & Co., 1938), p. 68.

14. John Dewey, *Essays in Experimental Logic* (Chicago: University of Chicago Press, 1916), p. 238.

15. John Dewey, *Art as Experience* (New York: G. P. Putnam's Sons, Capricorn Books, 1958), p. 58.

16. Dewey, *Essays in Experimental Logic*, p. 238.

17. Alfred Schutz and Thomas Luckmann, *The Structures of the Life-World* (Evanston, Ill.: Northwestern University Press, 1973), pp. 36–45.

18. John Dewey, *Democracy and Education* (New York: Macmillan Co., Free Press, 1966), p. 11.

19. John Wild, *Existence and the World of Freedom* (Englewood Cliffs, N.J.: Prentice-Hall, 1963), p. 47.

20. John Dewey, *Experience and Education* (New York: Macmillan Co., Collier Books, 1965), p. 43. Dewey also said: "An organism acts with reference to a time-spread, a serial order of events, as a unit, just as it does in reference to a unified spatial variety. Thus an environment both extensive and enduring is immediately implicated in present behavior. Operatively speaking, the remote and past are 'in' behavior, making it what it is. The action called 'organic' is not just that of internal structures; it is an integration of organic-environmental connections." *Experience and Nature*, p. 279. Dewey also observed that: "The thing essential to bear in mind is that living as an empirical affair is not something which goes on below the skin-surface of the organism: it is always an inclusive affair involving connection, interaction of what is within the organic body and what lies outside in space and time, and with higher organisms far outside." Ibid., p. 282.

21. John Dewey, "Address to Physicians," in Joseph Ratner, ed., *Intelligence in the Modern World* (New York: Random House, Modern Library, 1939), p. 821.

22. Dewey, *Democracy and Education*, p. 11.

23. Helmut R. Wagner, ed., *Alfred Schutz on Phenomenology and Social Relations: Selected Writings* (Chicago: University of Chicago Press, 1970), pp. 320, 14.

24. Maurice Natanson, *The Journeying Self: A Study in Philosophy and Social Role* (Reading, Mass.: Addison-Wesley Co., 1970), p. 95.

25. Schutz says of "radical pragmatism" that it is in error, because it interprets "the activities of consciousness . . . as actions in the outer world having exclusively practical aims, in particular aims designed to satisfy biological needs." *Reflections on Relevance*, p. 142.

26. Ibid., p. 169.

27. Dewey, *Democracy and Education*, p. 11.

28. For a related discussion which includes Schutz's use of the term "environment," see "Subject-Object Unification in Situation," in Chapter 5 of this study.

The question of whether or not Dewey was to be included in Schutz's criticism of pragmatism is an interesting and perplexing one. Richard Zaner and Mrs. Schutz have suggested that Schutz might not have had Dewey in mind when he criticized pragmatism, while Natanson believes that he did. If Schutz indeed wished Dewey included among the pragmatists he criticized, an explanation might be that there is little evidence Schutz ever read such books as *Art as Experience* and *Experience and Nature*. Yet these are the very texts which bring Dewey closest to Schutz's ideas. Schutz footnotes neither of these books in his writings, and an examination of his personal library (kindly made available to me by Mrs. Schutz) showed that Schutz owned only three books by Dewey: *Human Nature and Conduct: An Introduction to Social Psychology* (New York: Modern Library, 1930), *Logic*, and *Problems of Men*. The only other book by Dewey to which he refers in his writing (and that, only once) is *How We Think* (Chicago: Henry Regnery Co., 1971).

Natanson does not recall Schutz ever discussing these books. But he was quick to point out that it was characteristic of Schutz to immerse himself in the works of the philosophers he studied, and that it would be decidedly uncharacteristic of him not to have read all Dewey's major writings. Zaner reinforces this contention by saying that Schutz knew "practically all" Dewey's works and "certainly" *Art as Experience* and *Experience and Nature*. Zaner to author, 2 October 1972. Natanson to author, 25 September 1972.

If we assume that Schutz had read these books, we must live with the possibility that (a) he did not mean Dewey to be included in his criticism of pragmatism; (b) he misinterpreted Dewey (a possibility which I find unlikely, given Schutz's interests, unquestionable ability, and intellectual thoroughness); or (c) the argument presented here either misreads Dewey or misreads Schutz's criticism of pragmatism.

29. Schutz and Luckmann, *Structures of the Life-World*, p. 3.
30. James, *Principles of Psychology*, 2:299.
31. Schutz and Luckmann, *Structures of the Life-World*, p. 21.
32. Ibid., p. 24.
33. Schutz, "On Multiple Realities," in idem, *Collected Papers Vol. 1*, p. 230.
34. Schutz and Luckmann, *Structures of the Life-World*, p. 32.
35. Ibid., p. 26.
36. Ibid., p. 27.
37. Alfred Schutz, "Making Music Together," in idem, *Collected Papers Vol. 2: Studies in Social Theory*, ed. Arvid Brodersen (The Hague: Martinus Nijhoff, 1964), p. 171.
38. Schutz, "On Multiple Realities," in idem, *Collected Papers Vol. 1*, p. 207.
39. Schutz and Luckmann, *Structures of the Life-World*, p. 23.
40. Schutz, "Symbol, Reality and Society," in idem, *Collected Papers Vol. 1*, p. 344.
41. Schutz and Luckmann, *Structures of the Life-World*, p. 35.
42. Schutz, "On Multiple Realities," in idem, *Collected Papers Vol. 1*, p. 233.
43. Schutz, *Reflections on Relevance*, p. 126.
44. Zaner to author, 2 October 1972. Maurice Natanson takes another view and referred the author to the criticism of pragmatism found in *Collected Papers Vol. 1*, pp. 53, 213, as an example of Schutz's opposition to Dewey.
45. For Schutz's definition of "working acts," see "On Multiple Realities," in idem, *Collected Papers Vol. 1*, p. 212.
46. The power of this objectified social reality is not to be underestimated. Those who insist on the primacy of a personal reality beyond common reality not only find communication with others severely limited, but ipso facto are likely to be defined as mad.

John Dewey addressed this question by pointing out that: "Psychiatrists have made us familiar with disturbances labeled 'withdrawal from reality.' They have pointed out the role of this withdrawal in many pathological occurrences. What are these withdrawals but cases of the interruption or cessation of 'the active operative presence of environing conditions in the activities of a human being'? What are the resulting pathological phenomena but evidences that the self loses its integrity *within itself* when it loses integration with the medium in which it lives?" (Dewey's italics.) In Ratner, *Intelligence in the Modern World*, p. 824; from an address delivered before the College of Physicians in St. Louis on 21 April 1937. See also Dewey, *Experience and Nature,* p. 226; and idem, *Logic*, p. 106.

47. John Dewey, "Interpretation of the Savage Mind," in Joseph Ratner, ed., *John Dewey: Philosophy, Psychology, and Social Practice* (New York: G. P. Putnam's Sons, Capricorn Books, 1965), pp. 294, 281–82.

48. Ibid., p. 284.

49. Schutz, *Reflections on Relevance*, p. 125.

50. Schutz, "On Multiple Realities," in idem, *Collected Papers Vol. 1*, p. 233.

51. Schutz, "Husserl's Importance for the Social Sciences," in idem, *Collected Papers Vol. 1*, p. 148.

52. Dewey, "Interpretation of the Savage Mind," in Ratner, *John Dewey: Philosophy, Psychology, and Social Practice,* p. 287. It is significant to point out that Dewey was so indebted to W. I. Thomas for insight gained from conversations with him and from his writings, that he regarded the article as "virtually a joint contribution." Ibid., p. 287n5.

53. Ibid., p. 284. This suggested direction for sociology was undertaken to some degree in the early work of the Chicago school. Its emphasis was lost, however, as other systems of sociological analysis overshadowed it. Sixty years later, the call was raised again by Peter Berger and Thomas Luckmann. "We would contend that the linkage we have been led to make here between the sociology of knowledge and the theoretical core of the thought of Mead and his school suggests an interesting possibility for what might be called a sociological psychology, that is a psychology that derives its fundamental perspectives from a sociological understanding of the human condition." *Social Construction of Reality*, p. 186.

54. Wagner, *Alfred Schutz on Phenomenology and Social Relations*, p. 47n.

55. Dewey, *Art as Experience*, pp. 15, 78. Dewey makes a related point about man's religious nature. "The essentially unreligious attitude is that which attributes human achievement and purpose to man in isolation from the world of physical nature and his fellows. Our successes are dependent upon the co-operation of nature. The sense of the dignity of human nature is as religious as is the sense of awe and reverence when it rests upon a sense of human nature as a cooperating part of a larger whole." *A Common Faith* (New Haven, Conn.: Yale University Press, 1963), p. 25.

56. Dewey, *Experience and Nature*, p. 5.

57. Ibid.

58. Wild, *Existence and the World of Freedom*, p. 61.

59. Dewey, *Experience and Nature*, p. 16.

60. Dewey, *Art as Experience*, p. 3; see also idem, *Experience and Nature*, pp. 322–23.

61. Dewey, *Experience and Nature*, pp. 344–45.

62. Dewey discusses this issue in *Experience and Education*, p. 44.

63. James, *Principles of Psychology*, 2:301.

64. Bruce Wilshire, *William James and Phenomenology: A Study of the "Principles of Psychology"* (Bloomington: Indiana University Press, 1968), pp. 171–78.

65. Schutz, *Reflections on Relevance*, p. 8.

66. Ibid., p. 12.

67. Dewey, *Human Nature and Conduct*, pp. 40–41.

68. See Schutz, *Reflections on Relevance*, p. xviii.

69. Schutz, "On Multiple Realities," in idem, *Collected Papers Vol. 1*, p. 207; see also James, *Principles of Psychology*, 2:283–324.
70. See Zaner's introduction in Schutz, *Reflections on Relevance*, p. xv.
71. Ibid., pp. xix–xx.

Chapter 5

1. For an intriguing investigation of a man afflicted with near-total recall, see A. R. Luria, *The Mind of a Mnemonist*, trans. Lynn Solotaroff (New York: Basic Books, 1968).
2. John Dewey, "Experience, Knowledge and Value: A Rejoinder," in Paul Arthur Schilpp, ed., *The Philosophy of John Dewey* (Evanston and Chicago, Ill.: Northwestern University Press, 1939), p. 544.
3. For example, see Peter L. Berger, *Invitation to Sociology: A Humanistic Perspective* (Garden City, N.Y.: Doubleday & Co., Anchor Books, 1963), pp. 51–52, 54–65, especially on the topic of alternation.
4. John Dewey, *How We Think* (Chicago: Henry Regnery Co., 1971), p. 125.
5. John Dewey, *Experience and Nature*, 2d ed. (New York: Dover Publications, 1958), p. 311. Cf.: "The theme is, of course, always a theme within a field; each theme always has its specific horizon. Husserl has pointed out that horizon has a two-fold meaning: outer and inner horizon. *The outer horizon* is used to designate everything which occurs simultaneously with the theme in the actual field of consciousness. [It also designates] everything that refers by means of retentions and recollections to the genesis of the theme in the past. . . . On the other hand, there is the *inner horizon*. Once the theme has been constituted, it becomes possible to enter more . . . deeply (perhaps indefinitely) into its structure. . . ." Alfred Schutz, *Reflections on the Problem of Relevance*, ed. Richard M. Zaner (New Haven, Conn.: Yale University Press, 1970), pp. 30–31.
6. Alfred Schutz, "Some Leading Concepts in Phenomenology," in idem, *Collected Papers Vol. 1: The Problem of Social Reality*, ed. Maurice Natanson, 3d ed. (The Hague: Martinus Nijhoff, 1962), p. 108.
7. John Dewey, *Essays in Experimental Logic* (Chicago: University of Chicago Press, 1916), p. 6. Schutz makes a very similar point using almost the same example; see *Reflections on Relevance*, pp. 1–16.
8. "In more general terms, my motivational relevances are sedimentations of previous experiences, once typically or interpretationally relevant . . . to me, which led to a permanent habitual possession of knowledge—remaining dormant as long as the former topical relevances do not recur, but which become actualized if the 'same' situation or a typically similar one ('the same situation but modified,' 'a like situation,' 'a similar situation,' etc.) recurs." Schutz, *Reflections on Relevance*, p. 55.
9. John Dewey, *Art as Experience* (New York: G. P. Putnam's Sons, Capricorn Books, 1958), p. 264.
10. George Geiger has pointed out that "Dewey's use of this now familiar term ['field'] goes back to his earliest writings and may well antedate the general application of the word in physical theory." *John Dewey in Perspective* (New York: McGraw-Hill Book Co., 1964), p. 17. A similar claim was made by Dewey himself. See Schilpp, *Philosophy of John Dewey*.
11. John Dewey, *Logic: The Theory of Inquiry* (New York: Henry Holt & Co., 1938), p. 67. Schutz has said: "There is no such thing as an isolated ex-

perience. Any experience is experience within a context. Any present experience receives its meaning from the sum total of past experiences which led to the present one and is also connected by more or less empty anticipations to further experiences, the occurrence of which may or may not fulfill these expectations." *Reflections on Relevance*, p. 88.

12. Schutz, "Some Leading Concepts in Phenomenology," in idem, *Collected Papers Vol. 1*, p. 112. See also ibid., "Common-Sense and Scientific Interpretation of Human Action," p. 7; and ibid., "Language, Language Disturbances, and the Texture of Consciousness," pp. 279–80.

13. Schutz, "Some Leading Concepts in Phenomenology," in idem, *Collected Papers Vol. 1*, p. 112.

14. Dewey, *Experience and Nature*, p. 305. This seems to exempt Dewey from the charges Schutz leveled against "vulgar pragmatism." Describing this term, Schutz said: "With very few exceptions, vulgar pragmatism does not consider the problems of the constitution of conscious life involved in the notion of an *ego agens* or *homo faber* from which as a givenness most writers start. For the most part, pragmatism is, therefore, just a common-sense description of the attitude of man within the world of working in daily life, but not a philosophy investigating the pre-suppositions of such a situation." "On Multiple Realities," *Collected Papers Vol. 1*, p. 213n8.

Dewey moves into the problems of what constitutes the background of consciousness by two related routes. First, he believes that the taken-for-granted nature of the background must be penetrated by reflective analysis. This method is not equivalent to phenomenological bracketing, but that, of course, is not the issue. The point is only that Dewey doesn't assume the construction of consciousness as a mere "given." Second, and perhaps at greater divergence from phenomenology, Dewey believed that the route which leads to the background of human consciousness originates in foreground. "My 'metaphysical principle' is that the related foreground may be taken as a method for determining the traits of the background," he said. "Half-Hearted Naturalism," in Charles Morris, *Six Theories of Mind* (Chicago: University of Chicago Press, 1932), p. 327.

15. Helmut Kuhn, "The Phenomenological Concept of 'Horizon'," in Maurice Natanson, *The Journeying Self: A Study in Philosophy and Social Role* (Reading, Mass.: Addison-Wesley Co., 1970), p. 191.

16. Schutz, "Language, Language Disturbances, and the Texture of Consciousness," in idem, *Collected Papers Vol. 1*, p. 279.

17. John Dewey, *Democracy and Education* (New York: Macmillan Co., Free Press, 1966), p. 29. See also idem, *The Public and Its Problems* (Chicago: Swallow Press, 1954), p. 169.

18. Dewey, *Experience and Nature*, p. 280.

19. John-Paul Sartre, *Being and Nothingness*, trans. Hazel E. Barnes (New York: Philosophical Library, 1956), pp. 47–70. See also Berger, *Invitation to Sociology*, pp. 143–44, 147, 149; and Natanson, *Journeying Self*, p. 121.

20. Dewey, *Democracy and Education*, p. 339.

21. Kuhn, "Phenomenological Concept of 'Horizon'," in Natanson, *Journeying Self*, p. 191.

22. Dewey, *Experience and Nature*, p. 281.

23. Dewey's interest in scientific methods and education are understandable if we consider what has been said. Habits, as he understood them, could either form "ruts" which directed but limited consciousness, or they could provide roads which led men out into ever growing possibilities. Scientific method does not provide the only method for transcending the limits of habitual ruts, but for Dewey it was the most consistently useful method for achieving that goal.

See *Democracy and Education*, pp. 219–31. Education, he believed, "free[s] . . . individual capacity, . . . keeps alive a creative and constructive attitude," and liberates "human intelligence and human sympathy." *Logic*, pp. 115, 231, 269; quoted in Charles Morris, *The Pragmatic Movement in American Philosophy* (New York: George Braziller, 1970), p. 162. For further observations on habits, see also Dewey, *Democracy and Education*, p. 278; and idem, *The Public and Its Problems*, p. 167.

24. William James, *The Principles of Psychology*, 2 vols. (New York: Dover Publications, 1950), 1:488.

25. Anton Zijderveld, *The Abstract Society* (Garden City, N.Y.: Doubleday & Co., 1970), pp. 33–34. See also Peter L. Berger and Hansfried Kellner, "Arnold Gehlen and the Theory of Institutions," *Social Research* 32 (1965): 110–15; and Berger, *The Sacred Canopy* (Garden City, N.Y.: Doubleday & Co., Anchor Books, 1967), p. 19. John Dewey's notions on instincts are not dissimilar and are explained in Dewey, *Human Nature and Conduct: An Introduction to Social Psychology* (New York: Modern Library, 1930).

26. Jean Piaget, *The Construction of Reality in the Child*, trans. Margaret Cook (New York: Basic Books, 1954).

27. Schutz, *Reflections on Relevance*, p. 22.

28. Dewey, *Experience and Nature*, p. 303.

29. Dewey, *How We Think*, pp. 149–50.

30. Dewey, *Human Nature and Conduct*, p. 131.

31. Ibid., pp. 141–42.

32. Helmut R. Wagner, ed., *Alfred Schutz on Phenomenology and Social Relations: Selected Writings* (Chicago: University of Chicago Press, 1970), pp. 116–22.

33. Dewey, *Experience and Nature*, p. 219.

34. Dewey, *Essays in Experimental Logic*, p. 137; see also idem, *Democracy and Education*, p. 47.

35. Morris, *Pragmatic Movement in American Philosophy*, p. 4.

36. Dewey, *Democracy and Education*, pp. 291–305.

37. Alfred Schutz, "Equality and the Social Meaning Structure," in idem, *Collected Papers Vol. 2: Studies in Social Theory*, ed. Arvid Brodersen (The Hague: Martinus Nijhoff, 1964), p. 231.

38. Schutz, *Reflections on Relevance*, pp. 61–62.

39. Dewey, *Essays in Experimental Logic*, p. 139.

40. Schutz put it this way: "Familiarity thus indicates the likelihood of referring new experiences, in respect to their types, to the habitual stock of already acquired knowledge." *Reflections on Relevance*, pp. 58–59.

41. Dewey, *Essays in Experimental Logic*, pp. 144–45n1.

42. Dewey, *Experience and Nature*, pp. 290, 305–6.

43. Dewey, *Human Nature and Conduct*, pp. 75, 76, 41.

44. Schutz, *Reflections on Relevance*, p. 58.

45. Dewey, *Human Nature and Conduct*, p. 42.

46. Schutz, *Reflections on Relevance*, p. 62.

47. Dewey, *Human Nature and Conduct*, p. 177.

48. Ibid.

49. Schutz, *Reflections on Relevance*, p. 27. Sometimes the line of demarcation is anything but clear between background habits deemed unproblematic and foreground objects identified as problematic. At times, vast areas of the background are brought to our attention as problematic. This dislodgement can cause a great deal of disorientation. The time-consuming nature of psychoanalysis testifies that reorganization of background material can be a monu-

mental task. See Peter L. Berger, "Towards a Sociological Understanding of Psychoanalysis," *Social Research* 32 (1965): 26–41. Brainwashing techniques facilitate the disorientation of background and make it increasingly difficult for victims to hold anything as a warranted assertion. See Anselm L. Strauss, *Mirrors and Masks* (Mill Valley, Calif.: Sociology Press, 1969). We can assume that consciousness is threatened if a mind loses its structural coherence and order to such a degree that nothing can be taken for granted. As Dewey has said, panic accompanies such situations (*Logic*, p. 105); see also Schutz, "Equality and the Social Meaning Structure," in idem, *Collected Papers Vol. 2*, p. 231. Mental illness, however, is characterized not by lack of background but by a "distorted" background held together by its own form of logical connection (relevance structures). Communication in such cases becomes exceedingly difficult, because the patient does not share with others an inter-subjective background of understanding. See Gregory Bateson, *Steps to an Ecology of Mind* (New York: Ballantine Books, 1972).

The sociological conception of anomie describes situations in which the social world order collapses and is overrun by "lurking irrealities." Peter Berger defines the concept of nomos as "an edifice erected in the face of potent and alien forces of chaos." It amounts to a reality maintenance system. See Berger, *Sacred Canopy*, pp. 23–24. Individual consciousness and social order demand a nomonic structure which serves as a background in consciousness.

50. Dewey, *Experience and Nature*, p. 166.

51. Alfred Schutz, *The Phenomenology of the Social World*, trans. George Walsh and Frederick Lehnert (Evanston, Ill.: Northwestern University Press, 1967), p. 75.

52. Schutz, "Symbol, Reality and Society," in idem, *Collected Papers Vol 1.*, p. 356.

53. Dewey, *Experience and Nature*, p. 166.

54. Schutz, "Language, Language Disturbances, and the Texture of Consciousness," in idem, *Collected Papers Vol. 1*, p. 285.

55. Dewey, *How We Think*, p. 235.

56. Berger, *Sacred Canopy*, p. 4.

57. Dewey, *Experience and Nature*, pp. 166, 174.

58. Schutz, *Reflections on Relevance*, p. 154.

59. Dewey, *Experience and Nature*, pp. 166–207.

60. Schutz, "Choosing among Projects of Action," in idem, *Collected Papers Vol. 1*, pp. 67–96.

61. John Dewey, *Experience and Education* (New York: Macmillan Co., Collier Books, 1965), pp. 27, 77; see also idem, *Art as Experience*, p. 19.

62. T. S. Eliot, *Burnt Norton* (London: Faber & Faber, 1941), p. 9.

63. Dewey, *Experience and Education*, p. 37.

64. Dewey, *Experience and Nature*, pp. 258–59.

65. Peter L. Berger and Thomas Luckmann, *The Social Construction of Reality: A Treatise in the Sociology of Knowledge* (Garden City, N.Y.: Doubleday & Co., Anchor Books, 1967), p. 58.

66. Dewey, *Experience and Nature*, pp. 200, 196.

67. Quoted in Herbert Spiegelberg, *Phenomenology in Psychology and Psychiatry: Studies in Phenomenology and Existential Philosophy* (Evanston, Ill.: Northwestern University Press, 1972), p. 202.

68. John Dewey, "From Absolutism to Experimentalism," in Richard J. Bernstein, ed., *On Experience, Nature, and Freedom* (Indianapolis, Ind.: Bobbs-Merrill Co., Liberal Arts Press, 1960), p. 10.

69. Dewey, *Experience and Nature*, pp. 21, 268, 24.

70. Dewey, "Experience, Knowledge and Value," in Schilpp, *Philosophy of John Dewey*, p. 531.

71. Dewey, *Experience and Nature*, pp. x, 4a.

72. See Berger and Luckmann, *Social Construction of Reality*, pp. 60–61, 104. Berger and Luckmann point out that "the relationship between man, the producer, and the social world, his product, is and remains a dialectical one." Dewey comes to very similar conclusions, but he grounds this in the important relationship between man and nature.

73. Dewey, *Art as Experience*, p. 13; for the related issue of subjective versus objective analysis, see John Dewey and Arthur F. Bentley, *Knowing and the Known* (Boston: Beacon Press, 1949), pp. 103–8.

74. Dewey, *Democracy and Education*, p. 336.

75. Schutz, *Reflections on Relevance*, p. 37. Schutz said elsewhere that both topical and interpretive relevances "are situationally conditioned." Ibid., p. 43. The actual interest (motivational relevance) "of the subject is . . . dependent on the *circumstances* and the *situation* within which the problems have arisen. . . ." (Italics added.) Ibid., p. 28. Habits are not simply an outcome of "personal history . . . but also a function of the *actual circumstances, the situational setting* within which these habits have been formed. . . ." (Italics added.) Ibid., p. 27. "At any moment of my conscious life I find myself within the world, and my position in it . . . as it appears to me is what I call my situation within the world. I am therefore . . . always 'in situation.'" Ibid., p. 167.

76. See Dewey, *Logic*, p. 105; and idem, *How We Think*, p. 108.

77. Dewey, *Logic*, p. 106.

78. Schutz, *Reflections on Relevance*, pp. 4–5. "To be sure, a voluntary act is needed to perform [the] translation of horizonal material into topical terms, but this freedom is limited." Ibid., p. 34.

79. Quoted in Corliss Lamont, *Freedom of Choice Affirmed* (Boston: Beacon Press, 1969), p. 106.

80. Schutz, *Reflections on Relevance*, p. 4.

81. John Dewey, "The Reflex Arc Concept in Psychology," in Joseph Ratner, ed., *John Dewey: Philosophy, Psychology, and Social Practice* (New York: G. P. Putnam's Sons, Capricorn Books, 1965), p. 258.

82. Ibid., p. 255.

83. Schutz, *Reflections on Relevance*, p. 91.

84. Dewey, *Experience and Education*, p. 42. Schutz is making the same point and perhaps on a grander scale, when he insists that culture and man co-determine the makeup of an individual's life-world. See "Some Structures of the Life-World," in *Collected Papers Vol. 3: Studies in Phenomenological Philosophy*, ed. Ilse Schutz (The Hague: Martinus Nijhoff, 1966), pp. 119–20. Schutz said: "The individual living in the world always experiences himself as being within a certain situation which he has to define. Closer analysis shows that the concept of a situation to be defined contains two principal components: The one originates in the ontological structure of the pre-given world. The other . . . originates from the actual biographical state of the individual. . . ." Ibid., p. 122.

85. Dewey, *Logic*, p. 106.

86. Natanson, *Journeying Self*, p. 203.

87. Schutz, "Common-Sense and Scientific Interpretation," in idem, *Collected Papers Vol. 1*, p. 34.

88. Schutz, *Reflections on Relevance*, p. 91. Dewey makes the same point in a different way. Even when dealing with something as seemingly subjective as human expression, he points out that what is expressed is "neither the past

events that have exercised their shaping influence nor yet the literal existing occasion. It [is] in the degree of its spontaneity, an intimate union of the features of present existence with the values that past experiences have incorporated in personality. Immediacy and individuality, the traits that mark concrete existence, come from the present occasion; *meaning, substance, content,* from what is embedded in the self from the past." (Italics added.) *Art as Experience,* p. 71.

89. Dewey, "Psychology as Philosophical Method," in Schilpp, *Philosophy of John Dewey,* p. 269n12.

Chapter 6

1. Alfred Schutz, *The Phenomenology of the Social World,* trans. George Walsh and Frederick Lenhert (Evanston, Ill.: Northwestern University Press, 1967), p. 250.

2. Alfred Schutz, "Some Structures of the Life-World," in idem, *Collected Papers Vol. 3: Studies in Phenomenological Philosophy,* ed. Ilse Schutz (The Hague: Martinus Nijhoff, 1966), p. 123. "But the term 'interest' is simply a heading for a series of complicated problems, which for the sake of convenience shall be called the problem of *relevance.*" (Schutz's italics.) Idem, "Language, Language Disturbances, and the Texture of Consciousness," *Collected Papers Vol. 1: The Problem of Social Reality,* ed. Maurice Natanson, 3d ed. (The Hague: Martinus Nijhoff, 1962), p. 283.

3. Alfred Schutz, *Reflections on the Problem of Relevance,* ed. Richard M. Zaner (New Haven, Conn.: Yale University Press, 1970), pp. 55, 64–65.

4. Quoted in Jules Altman, Sidney Ratner, and James E. Wheeler, eds., *John Dewey and Arthur F. Bentley: A Philosophical Correspondence, 1932–1951* (New Brunswick, N.J.: Rutgers University Press, 1964), p. 242.

5. Alfred Schutz, "Tiresias, or Our Knowledge of Future Events," in idem, *Collected Papers Vol. 2: Studies in Social Theory,* ed. Arvid Brodersen (The Hague: Martinus Nijhoff, 1964), p. 288.

6. Schutz, "Language, Language Disturbances, and the Texture of Consciousness," in idem, *Collected Papers Vol. 1,* p. 278.

7. Ibid.

8. John Dewey, *Human Nature and Conduct: An Introduction to Social Psychology* (New York: Modern Library, 1930), p. 191.

9. John Dewey, *Experience and Nature,* 2d ed. (New York: Dover Publications, 1958), p. 421.

10. John Dewey, *Art as Experience* (New York: G. P. Putnam's Sons, Capricorn Books, 1958), pp. 13, 59–60.

11. Schutz, "Tiresias" in idem, *Collected Papers Vol. 2,* p. 288.

12. John Dewey, "Interest in Relation to Training of the Will," in Reginald Archamault, ed., *John Dewey on Education: Selected Writings* (New York: Random House, Modern Library, 1964), p. 273.

13. Schutz, "Some Structures of the Life-World," in idem, *Collected Papers Vol. 3,* p. 123.

14. Ibid., p. 122

15. Schutz, "Choosing among Projects of Action," in idem, *Collected Papers Vol. 1,* p. 77.

16. Ibid., p. 71.

17. Schutz, "Some Structures of the Life-World," in idem, *Collected Papers Vol. 3,* p. 131.

18. Schutz, "On Multiple Realities," in idem, *Collected Papers Vol. 1,* pp. 214–15.

19. Schutz, "Choosing among Projects of Action," in idem, *Collected Papers Vol. 1*, p. 71.

20. Schutz, *Phenomenology of the Social World*, p. 92.

21. Dewey, *Human Nature and Conduct*, p. 75.

22. John Dewey, *Democracy and Education* (New York: Macmillan Co., Free Press, 1966), p. 125; see also idem, "Interest in Relation to Training of the Will," in Archambault, *John Dewey on Education*, p. 271.

23. Dewey, "Interest in Relation to Training of the Will," in Archambault, *John Dewey on Education*, p. 269; see also John Dewey, *Theory of Valuation* (Chicago: University of Chicago Press, 1966), p. 17.

24. John Dewey, "Context and Thought," in Richard J. Bernstein, ed., *On Experience, Nature and Freedom* (Indianapolis, Ind.: Bobbs-Merrill Co., Liberal Arts Press, 1960), pp. 101, 103.

25. William James, *The Principles of Psychology*, 2 vols. (New York: Dover Publications, 1950), 1:417.

26. Schutz, *Reflections on Relevance*, p. 55.

27. Ibid., p. 65.

28. Schutz, *Phenomenology of the Social World*, p. 92.

29. Schutz, "The Social World and the Theory of Social Action," in idem, *Collected Papers Vol. 2*, p. 13.

30. Schutz, *Phenomenology of the Social World*, p. 39.

31. Schutz, "Some Structures of the Life-World," in idem, *Collected Papers Vol. 3*, p. 116.

32. Schutz, *Reflections on Relevance*, p. 22.

33. Schutz, "Language, Language Disturbances, and the Texture of Consciousness," in idem, *Collected Papers Vol. 1*, p. 278; and idem, "Type and Eidos in Husserl's Late Philosophy," in *Collected Papers Vol. 3*, p. 98.

34. Schutz, "Language, Language Disturbances, and the Texture of Consciousness," in idem, *Collected Papers Vol. 1*, p. 279.

35. Schutz, *Reflections on Relevance*, pp. 138–39.

36. Schutz, "Symbol, Reality and Society," in idem, *Collected Papers Vol. 1*, p. 297.

37. Dewey, *Art as Experience*, p. 52.

38. Ibid. See also idem, *Democracy and Education*, pp. 143–51; and idem, *Experience and Nature*, p. 326.

39. Dewey, *Human Nature and Conduct*, pp. 25, 42; see also ibid., p. 72.

40. Dewey, *Democracy and Education*, p. 48.

41. Dewey, *Art as Experience*, p. 53.

42. Dewey, "Qualitative Thought," in Bernstein, *On Experience, Nature and Freedom*, p. 188.

43. Dewey, *Art as Experience*, pp. 174, 177, 175.

44. Dewey, *Democracy and Education*, p. 145.

45. Helmut R. Wagner, ed., *Alfred Schutz on Phenomenology and Social Relations: Selected Writings* (Chicago: University of Chicago Press, 1970), pp. 321–22.

46. Maurice Natanson, "Alfred Schutz on Social Reality and Social Science," *Social Research* 35 (1968):240.

47. Dewey, "Qualitative Thought," in Bernstein, *On Experience, Nature and Freedom*, p. 181.

48. Natanson, "Alfred Schutz on Social Reality and Social Science," pp. 239–40; see also Aron Gurwitsch, *The Field of Consciousness*, Duquesne Studies, Psychological Series 2 (Pittsburgh: Duquesne University Press, 1964), pp. 342–43, 394–404.

49. Schutz, "On Multiple Realities," in idem, *Collected Papers Vol. 1*, p. 228.

50. Natanson, "Alfred Schutz on Social Reality and Social Science," p. 239.

51. Dewey, "Qualitative Thought," in Bernstein, *On Experience, Nature and Freedom*, p. 183.

52. Calvin O. Schrag, *Experience and Being* (Evanston, Ill.: Northwestern University Press, 1969), p. 94.

53. Dewey, *Art as Experience*, p. 42.

54. Ibid.

55. Schrag, *Experience and Being*, pp. 93, 94.

56. Dewey, "Qualitative Thought," in Bernstein, *On Experience, Nature and Freedom*, p. 182.

57. Peter L. Berger, *The Sacred Canopy* (Garden City, N.Y.: Doubleday & Co., Anchor Books, 1967), pp. 42–43.

58. It seems questionable to suggest that the fundamental anxiety is a silent partner in all the operations of relevance. Certainly, experience is possible prior to the recognition of death.

59. Victor Kestenbaum, "Dewey's Notion of Habit" (Ed.D. diss., Rutgers University, 1972), p. 54.

60. Dewey, "Qualitative Thought," in Bernstein, *On Experience, Nature and Freedom*, p. 184.

61. Ibid., p. 198.

62. Schutz, *Reflections on Relevance*, p. 25.

63. Dewey, "Qualitative Thought," in Bernstein, *On Experience, Nature and Freedom*, p. 197.

64. Dewey, *Art as Experience*, pp. 104, 87.

65. Dewey, *Democracy and Education*, pp. 340, 235.

66. Schutz, "Choosing among Projects of Action," in idem, *Collected Papers Vol. 1*, pp. 92–94.

67. Schutz, *Reflections on Relevance*, pp. 10, 11.

68. Events may occur in a manner that brings the habitual from horizon to theme. Breaking a pencil point, for example, makes the pencil problem thematic and at least temporarily interrupts the theoretical flow of thought.

69. Dewey, *Experience and Nature*, p. 303.

70. Schutz, "On Multiple Realities," in idem, *Collected Papers Vol. 1*, p. 208.

71. John Dewey, *Experience and Education* (New York: Macmillan Co., Collier Books, 1965), p. 43.

72. Dewey, *Art as Experience*, pp. 99, 98; see also idem, *Essays in Experimental Logic* (Chicago: University of Chicago Press, 1916), pp. 273–79.

73. Kestenbaum, "Dewey's Notion of Habit," p. 107.

74. John Dewey, *Logic: The Theory of Inquiry* (New York: Henry Holt & Co., 1938), p. 107.

75. Dewey, *Experience and Nature*, p. 23.

76. Dewey, *Art as Experience*, p. 89.

77. Schutz, "Phenomenology and the Social Sciences," in idem, *Collected Papers Vol. 1*, p. 112.

78. Schutz, "Some Leading Concepts of Phenomenology," in idem, *Collected Papers Vol. 1*, p. 113.

79. Schutz, "Some Structures of the Life-World," in idem, *Collected Papers Vol. 3*, p. 124.

80. Ibid.

81. Schutz, *Reflections on Relevance*, p. 25.

82. Ibid., p. 27; see also ibid., p. 77.

83. James, *Principles of Psychology*, 1:221–23. Both Dewey and Schutz refer to this distinction.

84. Schutz, *Reflections on Relevance*, pp. 28–33.

85. Dewey, *Logic*, p. 107.

86. Dewey, *How We Think* (Chicago: Henry Regnery Co., 1971), p. 109.

87. Dewey, *Logic*, p. 108.

88. Schutz, "Some Structures of the Life-World," in idem, *Collected Papers Vol. 3*, pp. 125, 127.

89. Schutz, *Reflections on Relevance*, p. 124.

90. John Dewey, "Theory of Valuation," in George R. Geiger, *John Dewey in Perspective* (New York: McGraw-Hill Book Co., 1964), p. 54.

91. Schutz, *Reflections on Relevance*, p. 124.

92. John Dewey, "Experience, Knowledge and Value," in Paul Arthur Schilpp, ed., *The Philosophy of John Dewey* (Evanston and Chicago, Ill.: Northwestern University Press, 1939), pp. 586–88.

93. Charles S. Peirce, *Charles S. Peirce: Selected Writings*, ed. Philip P. Wiener (New York: Dover Publications, 1958), p. 99; see also Dewey, *How We Think*, p. 114.

94. Schutz, *Reflections on Relevance*, p. 36.

95. Schutz, "Language, Language Disturbances, and the Texture of Consciousness," in idem, *Collected Papers Vol. 1*, p. 279.

96. Schutz, *Reflections on Relevance*, pp. 41–43.

97. Schutz, "Language, Language Disturbances, and the Texture of Consciousness," in idem, *Collected Papers Vol. 1*, pp. 279, 280.

98. Schutz, "The Problem of Rationality in the Social World," in idem, *Collected Papers Vol. 2*, p. 77.

99. Dewey, *Human Nature and Conduct*, p. 190.

100. Ibid., pp. 191, 193.

101. Schutz, "Choosing among Projects of Action," in idem, *Collected Papers Vol. 1*, p. 80.

102. Schutz, *Reflections on Relevance*, pp. 41, 42.

103. Dewey, *Logic*, p. 66.

Chapter 7

1. Max Weber, *The Methodology of the Social Sciences*, trans. Edward A. Shils and Henry A. Finch (New York: Macmillan Co., Free Press, 1949), p. 81.

2. Alfred Schutz, "Phenomenology and the Social Sciences," in idem, *Collected Papers Vol. 1: The Problem of Social Reality*, ed. Maurice Natanson, 3d ed. (The Hague: Martinus Nijhoff, 1962), p. 120.

3. Alfred Schutz, *The Phenomenology of the Social World*, trans. George Walsh and Frederick Lehnert (Evanston, Ill.: Northwestern University Press, 1967), pp. 4, 9.

4. Alvin W. Gouldner, *The Coming Crisis of Western Sociology* (New York: Basic Books, 1970), p. 490.

5. Quoted in Floyd W. Matson, *The Broken Image: Man, Science, and Society* (Garden City, N.Y.: Doubleday & Co., 1966), p. 36.

6. Quoted in Raymond Aron, *Main Currents in Sociological Thought*, 2 vols., trans. Richard Howard and Helen Weaver (Garden City, N.Y.: Doubleday & Co., 1968), 1:94.

7. Peter L. Berger, *Invitation to Sociology: A Humanistic Perspective* (Garden City, N.Y.: Doubleday & Co., Anchor Books, 1963), pp. 24–52.

8. Comte would find little solace in Weber's contention that sociology cannot supply psychological peace. It has been reported that when Weber talked to a friend about the desperation he experienced as he viewed society from a sociological perspective, his friend asked why he continued to do sociology. His answer is as cynical a statement as is likely to be found in sociological

literature: "Because," he said, "I want to know how much I can stand." Quoted in Peter L. Berger, "Sociology and Freedom," in Brigitte Berger, ed., *Readings in Sociology: A Biographical Approach* (New York: Basic Books, 1974), p. 499; see also idem, "Sociology and Freedom," *American Sociologist* 6 (February 1971):1–5.

9. Brigitte Berger, *Readings in Sociology*, p. 495.

10. John Dewey, *The Public and Its Problems* (Chicago: Swallow Press, 1954), pp. 9, 10. Dewey makes a similar argument in regard to psychoanalysis. "The treatment of sex by psycho-analysis is most instructive, for it flagrantly exhibits both the consequences of artificial simplification and the transformation of social results into psychic causes. Writers, usually male, hold forth on the psychology of women, as if they were dealing with a Platonic universal entity, although they habitually treat men as individuals, varying with structure and environment. They treat phenomena which are peculiarly symptoms of the civilization of the West at the present time as if they were the necessary effects of fixed native impulses of human nature . . . . [Psychology] sets up a hard-and-fast preordained class under which specific acts are subsumed, so that their own quality and originality are lost from view. This is why the novelist and the dramatist are so much more illuminating as well as more interesting commentators on conduct than the schematizing psychologist." *Human Nature and Conduct: An Introduction to Social Psychology* (New York: Modern Library, 1930), pp. 153, 155.

11. John Dewey, "The Need for a Recovery of Philosophy," in Richard J. Bernstein, ed., *On Experience, Nature and Freedom* (Indianapolis, Ind.: Bobbs-Merrill Co., Liberal Arts Press, 1960), p. 59.

12. John Dewey, *Logic: The Theory of Inquiry* (New York: Henry Holt & Co., 1938), p. 507.

13. Ibid.

14. Alfred Schutz, "The Social World and the Theory of Social Action," in idem, *Collected Papers Vol. 2: Studies in Social Theory*, ed. Arvid Brodersen (The Hague: Martinus Nijhoff, 1964), p. 7.

15. Schutz, *Phenomenology of the Social World*, p. 13.

16. Alfred Schutz and Thomas Luckmann, *The Structures of the Life-World* (Evanston, Ill.: Northwestern University Press, 1973), p. 183.

17. Schutz, *Phenomenology of the Social World*, p. 37.

18. Maurice Natanson, ed., *Philosophy of the Social Sciences: A Reader* (New York: Random House, 1963), p. 273.

19. Egon Bittner, "Objectivity and Realism in Sociology," in George Psathas, ed., *Phenomenological Sociology: Issues and Applications* (New York: John Wiley & Sons, 1973), p. 120.

20. Ibid., p. 123.

21. For a discussion of the phenomenon of privatization, see Anton Zijderveld, *The Abstract Society* (Garden City, N.Y.: Doubleday & Co., 1970); Peter L. Berger, "The Liberal as the Fall Guy," *Center Magazine* (July–August 1972), pp. 38–47; and Peter L. Berger, Brigitte Berger, and Hansfried Kellner, *The Homeless Mind: Modernization and Consciousness* (New York: Random House, 1973).

22. Alfred Schutz, *Reflections on the Problem of Relevance*, ed. Richard M. Zaner (New Haven, Conn.: Yale University Press, 1970), p. 74.

23. Ibid., pp. 71, 66.

24. John Dewey, *How We Think* (Chicago: Henry Regnery Co., 1971), pp. 115–16.

25. Dewey, "In Defense of the Theory of Inquiry," in Bernstein, *On Experience, Nature and Freedom*, p. 134.

Selected Bibliography

Books by John Dewey

Dewey, John. *Essays in Experimental Logic.* Chicago: University of Chicago Press, 1916.
———. *A Common Faith.* New Haven, Conn.: Yale University Press, 1963.
———. *The Public and Its Problems.* Chicago: Swallow Press, 1954.
———. *Experience and Nature.* 2d ed. New York: Dover Publications, 1958.
———. *Human Nature and Conduct: An Introduction to Social Psychology.* New York: Modern Library, 1930.
———. *Individualism Old and New.* New York: G. P. Putnam's Sons, Capricorn Books, 1962.
———. *Philosophy and Civilization.* Gloucester, Mass.: Peter Smith, 1968.
———. *Art as Experience.* New York: G. P. Putnam's Sons, Capricorn Books, 1958.
———. *Logic: The Theory of Inquiry.* New York: Henry Holt & Co., 1938.
———. *The Influence of Darwin on Philosophy: And Other Essays in Contemporary Thought.* New York: Peter Smith, 1951.
———. *The Quest for Certainty.* New York: G. P. Putnam's Sons, Capricorn Books, 1960.
———. *Experience and Education.* New York: Macmillan Co., Collier Books, 1965.
———. *Democracy and Education.* New York: Macmillan Co., Free Press, 1966.
———. *Theory of Valuation.* Chicago: University of Chicago Press, 1966.
———. *How We Think.* Chicago: Henry Regnery Co., 1971.
———. *Problems of Men.* New York: Philosophical Library, 1946.
———, et al. *Creative Intelligence: Essays in the Pragmatic Attitude.* New York: Henry Holt & Co., 1917.
———, and Bentley, Arthur F. *Knowing and the Known.* Boston: Beacon Press, 1949.

Articles by John Dewey

Dewey, John. "The Objectivism-Subjectivism of Modern Philosophy." *Journal of Philosophy* 38 (1941):533–42.

Edited Collections of Articles, Essays, and Letters by John Dewey

Altman, Jules; Ratner, Sidney; and Wheeler, James E., eds. *John Dewey and Arthur F. Bentley: A Philosophical Correspondence, 1932–1951.* New Brunswick, N.J.: Rutgers University Press, 1964.

Archambault, Reginald, ed. *John Dewey on Education: Selected Writings*. New York: Random House, Modern Library, 1964.
Bernstein, Richard J., ed. *On Experience, Nature and Freedom*. Indianapolis, Ind.: Bobbs-Merrill Co., Liberal Arts Press, 1960.
Ratner, Joseph, ed. *Intelligence in the Modern World*. New York: Random House, Modern Library, 1939.
————, ed. *John Dewey: Philosophy, Psychology, and Social Practice*. New York: G. P. Putnam's Sons, Capricorn Books, 1965.

Books and Articles about John Dewey

Bernstein, Richard J. *John Dewey*. Great American Thinkers Series. New York: Washington Square Press, 1966.
Geiger, George R. *John Dewey in Perspective*. New York: McGraw-Hill Book Co., 1964.
Kestenbaum, Victor. "An Interpretation of Dewey's Notion of Habit from the Perspective of Merleau-Ponty's Phenomenology of the Habitual Body." Ed.D. dissertation. Rutgers University, 1972.
Roth, Robert J. *John Dewey and Self-Realization*. Englewood Cliffs, N.J.: Prentice-Hall, 1962.
Schilpp, Paul Arthur, ed. *The Philosophy of John Dewey*. Evanston and Chicago, Ill.: Northwestern University Press, 1939.

Books by Alfred Schutz

Schutz, Alfred. *The Phenomenology of the Social World*. Translated by George Walsh and Frederick Lehnert. Evanston, Ill.: Northwestern University Press, 1967.
————. *Reflections on the Problem of Relevance*. Edited by Richard M. Zaner. New Haven, Conn.: Yale University Press, 1970.
————, and Luckmann, Thomas. *The Structures of the Life-World*. Evanston, Ill.: Northwestern University Press, 1973.

Articles by Alfred Schutz

Schutz, Alfred. "The Social World and the Theory of Social Action." *Social Research* 27 (1960): 203–21.

Edited Collections of Articles and
Essays by Alfred Schutz

Schutz, Alfred. *Collected Papers Vol. 1: The Problem of Social Reality*. 3d ed. Edited and introduced by Maurice Natanson. The Hague: Martinus Nijhoff, 1962.
————. *Collected Papers Vol. 2: Studies in Social Theory*. Edited and introduced by Arvid Brodersen. The Hague: Martinus Nijhoff, 1964.
————. *Collected Papers Vol. 3: Studies in Phenomenological Philosophy*. Edited by Ilse Schutz and introduced by Aron Gurwitsch. The Hague: Martinus Nijhoff, 1966.
Wagner, H. R., ed. *Alfred Schutz on Phenomenology and Social Relations: Selected Writings*. Chicago: University of Chicago Press, 1970.

Books and Articles about
Alfred Schutz

Natanson, Maurice. "Alfred Schutz on Social Reality and Social Science." *Social Research* 35 (1968):217–44.
———. "The Phenomenology of Alfred Schutz." *Inquiry* 9 (1966):147–55.
———. *Phenomenology and Social Reality: Essays in Memory of Alfred Schutz.* The Hague: Martinus Nijhoff, 1970.

General Books

Aron, Raymond. *Introduction to the Philosophy of History.* Boston: Beacon Press, 1961.
———. *Main Currents in Sociological Thought.* 2 vols. Translated by Richard Howard and Helen Weaver. Garden City, N.Y.: Doubleday & Co., 1968.
Bateson, Gregory. *Steps to an Ecology of Mind.* New York: Ballantine Books, 1972.
Becker, Ernest. *Beyond Alienation.* New York: George Braziller, 1967.
Berger, Brigitte, ed. *Readings in Sociology: A Biographical Approach.* New York: Basic Books, 1974.
Berger, Peter L. *Invitation to Sociology: A Humanistic Perspective.* Garden City, N.Y.: Doubleday & Co., Anchor Books, 1963.
———. *The Sacred Canopy.* Garden City, N.Y.: Doubleday & Co., Anchor Books, 1967.
———, and Luckmann, Thomas. *The Social Construction of Reality: A Treatise in the Sociology of Knowledge.* Garden City, N.Y.: Doubleday & Co., Anchor Books, 1967.
———; Berger, Brigitte; and Kellner, Hansfried. *The Homeless Mind: Modernization and Consciousness.* New York: Random House, 1973.
Berlin, Isaiah. *The Age of Enlightenment: The Eighteenth Century Philosophers.* Great Ages of Western Philosophy Series, vol. 4 of 6 vols. Freeport, N.Y.: Books for Libraries Press, 1970.
Embree, Lester E., ed. *Life-World and Consciousness: Essays for Aron Gurwitsch.* Evanston, Ill.: Northwestern University Press, 1972.
Farber, Marvin. *Naturalism and Subjectivism.* Albany: State University of New York Press, 1968.
Gouldner, Alvin W. *The Coming Crisis of Western Sociology.* New York: Basic Books, 1970.
Gurwitsch, Aron. *The Field of Consciousness.* Duquesne Studies, Psychological Series 2. Pittsburgh: Duquesne University Press, 1964.
Husserl, Edmund. *Cartesian Meditations: An Introduction to Phenomenology.* Translated by Dorion Cairns. The Hague: Martinus Nijhoff, 1960.
James, William. *Essays in Radical Empiricism.* New York: Longmans, Green & Co., 1912.
———. *The Principles of Psychology.* 2 vols. New York: Dover Publications, 1950.
Kaufman, Felix. *Methodology of the Social Sciences.* New York: Oxford University Press, 1944.
Lamont, Corliss. *Freedom of Choice Affirmed.* Boston: Beacon Press, 1969.
Luckmann, Thomas. *The Invisible Religion.* New York: Macmillan Co., 1970.
Luria, A. R. *The Mind of a Mnemonist.* Translated by Lynn Solotaroff. New York: Basic Books, 1968.
Mathur, D. C. *Naturalistic Philosophies of Experience.* St. Louis, Mo.: Warren H. Green, 1971.

Matson, Floyd W. *The Broken Image: Man, Science, and Society.* Garden City, N.Y.: Doubleday & Co., 1966.

Merleau-Ponty, Maurice. *Phenomenology of Perception.* Translated by Colin Smith. New York: Humanities Press, 1962.

Morgenbesser, Sidney; Suppes, Patrick; and White, Morton, eds. *Philosophy, Science, and Method: Essays in Honor of Ernest Nagel.* New York: St. Martin's Press, 1969.

Morris, Charles. *The Pragmatic Movement in American Philosophy.* New York: George Braziller, 1970.

———. *Six Theories of Mind.* Chicago: University of Chicago Press, 1932.

Natanson, Maurice. *The Social Dynamics of George H. Mead.* Washington, D.C.: Public Affairs Press, 1956.

———. *The Journeying Self: A Study in Philosophy and Social Role.* Reading, Mass.: Addison-Wesley Co., 1970.

———, ed. *Literature, Philosophy, and the Social Sciences: Essays in Existentialism and Phenomenology.* The Hague: Martinus Nijhoff, 1968.

———, ed. *Philosophy of the Social Sciences: A Reader.* New York: Random House, 1963.

Ortega y Gasset, José. *Man and People.* New York: W. W. Norton & Co., 1963.

Peirce, Charles S. *Charles S. Peirce: Selected Writings.* Edited by Philip P. Wiener. New York: Dover Publications, 1958.

Piaget, Jean. *The Construction of Reality in the Child.* Translated by Margaret Cook. New York: Basic Books, 1954.

Psathas, George, ed. *Phenomenological Sociology: Issues and Applications.* New York: John Wiley & Sons, 1973.

Salomon, Albert. *The Tyranny of Progress: Reflections on the Origins of Sociology.* New York: Noonday Press, 1955.

Sartre, Jean-Paul. *Being and Nothingness.* Translated by Hazel E. Barnes. New York: Philosophical Library, 1956.

Schrag, Calvin O. *Experience and Being.* Evanston, Ill.: Northwestern University Press, 1969.

Spiegelberg, Herbert. *The Phenomenological Movement: A Historical Introduction.* 2 vols. 2d ed. The Hague: Martinus Nijhoff, 1971.

———. *Phenomenology in Psychology and Existential Philosophy: Studies in Phenomenology and Existential Philosophy.* Evanston, Ill.: Northwestern University Press, 1972.

Scheler, Max. *Man's Place in Nature.* Translated by Hans Meyerhoff. New York: Farrar, Straus & Cudahy, Noonday Press, 1969.

Strauss, Anselm L. *Mirrors and Masks.* Mill Valley, Calif.: Sociology Press, 1969.

Thomas, W. I. *The Child in America.* New York: Alfred A. Knopf, 1928.

Turnbull, Colin. *The Mountain People.* New York: Simon & Schuster, 1972.

von Mises, Ludwig. *Human Action.* London: William Hodge, 1949.

Watson, John B. *Behaviorism.* Chicago: University of Chicago Press, Phoenix Books, 1958.

Weber, Max. *The Methodology of the Social Sciences.* Translated by Edward A. Shils and Henry A. Finch. New York: Macmillan Co., Free Press, 1949.

Wild, John. *Existence and the World of Freedom.* Englewood Cliffs, N.J.: Prentice-Hall, 1963.

———. *The Radical Empiricism of William James.* Garden City, N.Y.: Doubleday & Co., 1969.

Wilshire, Bruce. *William James and Phenomenology: A Study of the "Principles of Psychology."* Bloomington: Indiana University Press, 1968.

Woodworth, Robert. *Contemporary Schools of Psychology.* New York: Ronald Press, 1948.

Zijderveld, Anton. *The Abstract Society.* Garden City, N.Y.: Doubleday & Co., 1970.

General Articles

Berger, Peter L. "Towards a Sociological Understanding of Psychoanalysis." *Social Research* 32 (1965):26–41.

———. "The Liberal as the Fall Guy." *Center Magazine,* July–August 1972, pp. 38–47.

———. "Sociology and Freedom." *American Sociologist* 6 (February 1971): 1–5.

———, and Kellner, Hansfried. "Arnold Gehlen and the Theory of Institutions." *Social Research* 32 (1965):110–15.

Heap, James L., and Roth, Phillip A. "On Phenomenological Sociology." *American Sociological Review* 38 (1973):354–67.

Natanson, Maurice. "Being-in-Reality." *Philosophy and Phenomenological Research* 20 (1959):231–37.

UNIVERSITY OF FLORIDA MONOGRAPHS

Social Sciences